Comedy

Comedy

Book Three
Secular Revelations

Patrick McGee

RESOURCE *Publications* · Eugene, Oregon

COMEDY, BOOK THREE
Secular Revelations

Copyright © 2024 Patrick McGee. All rights reserved. Except for brief quotations in critical publications or reviews, no part of this book may be reproduced in any manner without prior written permission from the publisher. Write: Permissions, Wipf and Stock Publishers, 199 W. 8th Ave., Suite 3, Eugene, OR 97401.

Resource Publications
An Imprint of Wipf and Stock Publishers
199 W. 8th Ave., Suite 3
Eugene, OR 97401

www.wipfandstock.com

PAPERBACK ISBN: 979-8-3852-1960-5
HARDCOVER ISBN: 979-8-3852-1961-2
EBOOK ISBN: 979-8-3852-1962-9

06/07/24

CONTENTS

Preface | *vii*

Canto 1	| 1		Canto 18	| 90
Canto 2	| 6		Canto 19	| 95
Canto 3	| 11		Canto 20	| 100
Canto 4	| 16		Canto 21	| 105
Canto 5	| 21		Canto 22	| 110
Canto 6	| 26		Canto 23	| 115
Canto 7	| 31		Canto 24	| 121
Canto 8	| 36		Canto 25	| 127
Canto 9	| 42		Canto 26	| 132
Canto 10	| 47		Canto 27	| 138
Canto 11	| 52		Canto 28	| 143
Canto 12	| 58		Canto 29	| 148
Canto 13	| 63		Canto 30	| 153
Canto 14	| 69		Canto 31	| 158
Canto 15	| 74		Canto 32	| 163
Canto 16	| 79		Canto 33	| 169
Canto 17	| 84			

Notes | 175

PREFACE

SECULAR REVELATIONS IS THE THIRD and final book of *Comedy*. Like the first two books, it largely consists of a series of dialogues. Though the concept of paradise is a recurring motif throughout this work, it diverges from Dante's concept in the *Paradiso* because it is not a transcendent place but a human experience that can be addressed and defined in multiple ways. The reader will find this book more personal than the first two, with fewer canonical figures and more personal contacts, though here and there the two categories overlap. The reader may notice an evolution from fairly formal language in the first book to increasingly more common language in the second and third books. References to cinematic culture carry over here from the second book, though not to the same degree. Woven into these are references and allusions to popular music from the blues to rock-and-roll.

As in the second book, I have included a set of notes at the end. Since this book gives primacy to real locations, the notes for each canto begin with a reference to the place or places in which the dialogues occur. Then follows the listing of any historical figures who participate in the dialogues. As in the second book, I then list the films referenced if there are any. After that come the general notes, including any references to popular music. In most cases, I only give the source of the reference or citation unless I feel it necessary to quote some lines. Occasionally, I alter the format in obvious ways in the interest of economy. The references to music are not exhaustive, and the reader may encounter allusions to songs in common phrases that pass unnoted.

I owe an enormous debt to my friends Robert Con Davis-Undiano and Tim Fitzmaurice. Both have been faithful readers of each canto as I wrote them. Their criticism and encouragement kept me going, and their own creative work has inspired me. I also appreciate the generous encouragement of Laura Haigwood. To my wife, Joan Rey Lara Espey McGee, I

Preface

dedicate this work. She is the "amorous revolution" that changed my life. The debt I owe to my mother, Lillian McGee, should be apparent in the work itself.

CANTO 1

Along Union Avenue with Phyllis DePriest,
I walked through memories of what had ceased
To exist, and though there was some loss of beauty—

For the ground had been cleared by forces of history—
Barrenness was the right valedictory
To a world that was and still is unforgiving,

That made poverty a sin against the living,
Though real life became the music of the poor
When Furry Lewis opened another door

And Bukka White followed and there were more,
White and black, back when Beale Street learned to talk,
But now Beale Street is an amusement park

Like New Orleans for people on a lark.
As we walked past Sun Records, all the times
I passed it by, paying the site no mind,

Made me think of things missed and left behind.
We reached the ground where long had stood the statue
Of Nathan Bedford Forrest, the man who

Gave legitimacy to the racist crew,
Then distanced himself from the evil he unleashed,
As if he knew how history would impeach

The terrorism of cowards in white sheets
Who thought all black people afraid of ghosts
And would be coerced to sacrifice their votes,

But it wasn't ghosts they feared but the use of ropes
That turned the desire for freedom into strange fruit
Hanging from trees in which hatred took root

With fibers whose spread had the power to pollute
The souls of white folks until they saw hell
As heaven and enclosed themselves in a shell

Comedy, Book Three

That shut out the light in which free souls dwell.
"Memphis has two souls," I said to Phyllis,
"But back then it was the beautiful one I missed,

Even though it was so close it almost kissed
My world, like when I worked at the Last Laugh
Where three nights a week I drew endless drafts

Of beer, while the most unlikely cenotaph
Of the blues was across the street at Peanuts' bar,
Because Furry Lewis played his guitar

There on Sunday nights, but the curmudgeon tsar
Of the place had been my boss over on Highland—
He looked like a Firbolg from mythical Ireland,

Like a bagman who never could give a damn
About blues unless it put cash in his hand—
So I stayed away from the place until one night

I crossed over to see the incredible sight
Of an old black bluesman who picked with a bottleneck
Slide that made the guitar weep over the wreck

Of human lives, yet kept the sadness in check
With a wit that said—'I ain't what they beat down,
And I ain't here to entertain folks like a clown,

And I know you don't know the truth of my sound,
But I'll play and drink whiskey until this town
Buries me deeper than they buried the blues,

Like those white singers who took my sound and used
It to get rich while mine was the voice of the poor
And I tried hard not to feel the need for more,

But I don't like white stars coming to my door,
Acting like they know me, thinking I'm funny,
Then going off to make a lotta money

Canto 1

Pretending to feel the things that got on me
From blind injustice in Memphis, Tennessee.'—
But that voice is just my imagination

Of what I missed in that secular revelation,
And who knows if it has any relation
To the mind that lay behind Furry's picking?"

"In life," Phyllis said, "desires are conflicting
And blind us to the truth of our own song,
Though others may sing it after we're gone,

And maybe forget how often we were wrong.
Everyone has their own form of the blues
But it took the poor to write music that woos

The heart of multitude with simple truths
About all the loves we won, lost, and betrayed
And the cruelty of the social masquerade

That would trump justice with power and then upbraid
The poor for creating a paradise in sound
To lift up all those who have been put down

And threaten power with passion unbound."
As we kept walking, we turned north on Cleveland
And she continued, "Sensations that sweetened

Our existence may sometimes have cheapened
The lives of others, back when we were rebels—
Or so we thought—though inside we were miserable

And answered the call of anything pleasurable,
Anything that shot us up to the stars—
Sex, booze, drugs, and the wild riffs of guitars,

In the dark musty paradise of the bars—
Though in upright Memphis we called them joints
Before liquor by the drink arrived to anoint

Comedy, Book Three

Our anesthetized souls to the furthest point
Of intoxication, the fabrication
Of synthetic ecstasies, stimulations

That soon brought about our separations,
For our loves, our friendships, were self-destructive,
And we had to fight against a force seductive,

Like electricity through spaces nonconductive
Arcing across souls, reducing to ashes
Tender emotions that too much love smashes

Until nothing's left but anger and clashes.
Joni Mitchell's was the voice that filled my void
But telling me I sang like her destroyed

The feeling of being myself and annoyed
The hell out of me, and that's one thing you did
Back then that caused my love for you to skid

Off the road and see you like a clueless kid,
But you just wanted to tell it like it is,
And that's what Joni did to Furry that pissed

Him off, when she sang of meeting him and dissed
His voice as mumbling—to him that song was a gun
Aimed at his head that said he was no one,

Like the carcass of Beale Street she called carrion.
She didn't mean to hurt and neither did you,
But the thing is, there's no justice in feeling blue,

Unless we make it into a song that's true,
And judges would be in a penitentiary too
If they had justice, like Furry sang way back,

And if there were justice he wouldn't have lacked
The wealth he needed to pursue his art,
He wouldn't have had to pawn his old guitar,

Canto 1

He wouldn't have had to push a broom and a cart,
He wouldn't have spent years not feeling a part
Of the world old bluesmen like him had created,

He wouldn't have felt the song of himself negated
By millionaire singers who relegated
The history of soul to a curiosity shop,

And the ones who sang it first wouldn't've been props
Used by corporate moguls to legitimate pop.
But that doesn't mean Joni's blues didn't matter,

When it flowed like blood from the heart deep inside her,
And the same is true for the Stones and Mick Jagger
And the different beats of hip hop and the rappers.

Behind rock and roll blues is the master,
But it's not just twelve bars and four-four time,
Just like poetry can't be defined by rhyme.

When music lifts pain up to realms sublime,
That's the paradise of the blues, like when
In Mobile the universal spoke to Dylan

Who named it Memphis, or to his mother Lennon
Cried out the pain buried in twist and shout
And leaving the Beatles he let it all hang out.

It's no accident the blues came from down south,
Where the soul that stole away from a black man's mouth
Became the voice of generations whose debt

Has yet to be paid but must without regret
One day come to pass for the good of all,
Because that voice has become universal,

A revelation to those who heed its call."

CANTO 2

We came to the corner of Cleveland and Madison,
And where once I'd thrived was now a dead zone
Because the places and people I loved were gone,

Though back then we would've said, "Been down so long,
It seems like up," but up meant mostly drunk,
When from the southern world we were disjunct,

And from the southern man Neal Young debunked,
But when Furry sang, *if the river was whiskey*,
Drunk he'd always be, we heard our misery

That found its momentary delivery
From the white man's hell into the false paradise
That let us all forget we were parodies

Of the revolution against cruel inequities
To which we, the children of the working class,
Pledged ourselves, though desire was the impasse,

The will to be something more, to surpass
The destiny shaped by the streets of this city
That like a maze without exit or pity

Trapped us in the blind sense of our futility.
"Stop!" Phyllis said, interrupting the flow
Of my mind's self-negation. "You swing too low,

And forget good things from that time long ago.
Your mind's open to me because that's where
I live, among other places, and your care

For me and others comes from love we share,
Not past but present, because love never dies.
We who are dead no longer deem it wise

To obsess over loss and then ourselves chastise
Because we failed to become the world's heroes.
Yes, sometimes we drank too much and then froze

Canto 2

When obstacles appeared on every road
That seemed to point toward something beyond
The immediate world that could never correspond

To the visionary dream that was our bond.
I was the first to give up that fantasy,
Not because I thought it such a travesty,

But I knew I had to find my own destiny,
My own sense of what it meant to be me,
And in myself being's collectivity,

Which doesn't make me part of the bourgeoisie,
But knowledge is the collective force that blasts
Open the walls that keep us bound to a class—

The voice of others congealed into a mass
That incorporates the living and the dead,
A singular event inside the head,

A mental tree whose roots shoot out and spread
To other minds that intertwine and shape
A new humanity that comes awake

To the common soul in which we all partake.
Our revolution was love of the common,
The force we saw in each other, the daemon

Of collective genius that some called a demon
Because through our mutual love we became
Other, and never more would be the same

Once we had touched each other with the flame
Of common desire that nothing can put out.
You look around this place and see a drought

Of spirit that makes you step back and doubt—
Does the life you knew survive in this wasteland?
But it survives in the power of mind to expand

Comedy, Book Three

If you'll only give yourself the command.
Then a cell in your brain will deliver you to a place—
Not the desiccated past to retrace

But to conjure the messianic event that creates
Concrete fragments of infinite being
That push beyond the space of finite seeing."

Pointing north by northeast, she said, "Freeing
Himself from time Furry plucked his tensed strings
Over there, but for you the music springs

From a different source but still gives you the wings
To fly through mental skies toward the sunrise
On a world where the thing deemed impossible thrives

Since whatever the heart embraces forever survives."
Then she pointed westward and something awoke
In my mind that gave me the power to invoke

A presence I thought temporal law had revoked.
Phyllis said, "You forgot you're in a dream
And took the traces of visions lately seen

As more than projections on a mental screen.
Since you opened a door of perception
On your walk, the iron logic of succession

In events has undergone a taut flexion
Like a möbius strip, with past and present folded
Into one another, and time remolded

Into the infinite now that has exploded
The dull round of predictable cause and effect."
Her words gave me the power to accept

The vision toward which I now had to direct
My steps—it was a place of communion,
Where a band of misplaced Memphis bohemians

Canto 2

Made themselves into a church of comedians
And laughter into a sacramental act
That blessed the beer we drank at The Last Laugh,

A name that became the proper epigraph
To the joint that bore our hidden society,
Bacchants of intoxicated sobriety.

I turned to Phyllis who said, "Undeniably,
Beyond that door lies a remembered space
Symbolic that no amount of time can erase,

Something past present the truth of which awaits
The future imperfect of ever expanding process.
Just as you remember me as not less

But more than what I was, a work in progress,
Even in death—expect sights unforeseen
That make your trip more than a time machine."

I opened the door and we entered a scene
That was the same yet different from the past
I once knew, and at the bar on which I cast

My eyes were shadowfolk whose images clashed
With my memory—then to the left I saw
My old friend Tom and heard his loud guffaws

As he played shuffleboard, when for some strange cause
He turned toward me and looked without a sign
Of recognition as if I'd been consigned

To invisibility, or the dark made blind
Those who should have known me—like the woman
Who wanted my love after I'd met the one

Who at the sight of her sculpted head had won
My heart and kept it enfolded in her own,
But this woman from the past could not see me,

Comedy, Book Three

Like the others who mirrored faded memory.
I looked to Phyllis who said, "These folks aren't dead,
 Or not yet living forces in your head,

 But another comes of whom you've often said,
 Not keeping in touch with her was a blind act
 Of stupidity that showed an utter lack

 Of understanding what time won't give back
 Of true friendship that never let you down
 Until you let forgetfulness it confound."

From the back of the place a person turned around
And the mere sight of her caused my heart to bound.
Pat Smith, looking as she did so many years

 Ago, brought to my eyes estatic tears
 And of her judgment perhaps one or two fears.
She approached us and said, "You don't need to cry,

 Though when you left I thought you'd surely try
To remember those who pulled you from despond's
 Sinkhole, for friendship is a singular bond

 That more than passionate love can go beyond
 Self-interest, because it never seeks fusion,
 Which often leads to heartbreak and confusion

 When romantic love generates the illusion
That the void between two souls can ever be closed.
I know in your heart our friendship keeps its hold

Though despite your searching you haven't been told
 If I'm alive or dead, but don't feel dread
 Over such a loss, the unbreakable thread

 That connects us keeps me alive in your head."

CANTO 3

Pat and I went to a table and sat down
While Phyllis stayed at the bar where spirits abound
Because in the world of the dead she has some renown—

For all the souls who knew her gave her a crown—
But across my face my heart painted a frown,
And Pat said, "Why must you always confound

Yourself with regret?—I know why you left this town,
A Charybdis chasm in which you thought you'd drown,
And the jukebox beckoned with The Animals' sound—

Gotta get out of this place before you're ground
Down until nothing's left to give you hope,
No way to escape the invisible hangman's rope

That leaves the spirit with a pinhead's scope
And the body broken without a mind to cope.
But there was a Memphis soul you couldn't escape,

Something you loved and could never forsake
And it became in you the will to create,
To forge infinite beauty and annihilate

All the finite covers that seek to negate
The love of multitude you associate
With this symbolic place where you first dreamed

Yourself into a being beyond what seemed
Worthless existence—where you touched bottom
But then looked up and saw something awesome,

The light of friendship, the essence of the common,
Powered by mutual forgiveness and love.
For without forgiveness existence is rough,

Dominated by fools who think they're tough,
But their concept of power is only a bluff
To hide from themselves the others who live inside,

Comedy, Book Three

The infinite part you can never divide
Into self and other, us and them, or black
And white—since already you'd found in William Blake

A mental presence in which you would partake
When he spoke to you as angels spoke to him,
Which wasn't madness or a holy whim

But a brain force that said forgiveness of sin
Is a portal of discovery, error
Creates progression while inflicting terror

On passive minds that block the human sharer
Who expands intellect into power divine
Because it blasts the subterfuge of time.

Thought is never property but sublime
Collectivity that forces cooperation
And builds a new paradise from the negation

Of fear that hides behind the wall of nation."
"How I miss the joy of conversation
With you," I said, "another education

Because you saw through the veils of sensation
People project to hide the unnamable
From others, the thing in themselves impassable,

Unavoidable, even though unknowable—
Beyond identity, nationality,
Yes, beyond any concept of property—

But you saw in its essence, its poverty,
A fullness of being to which you gave
Indirect expression with the power to save

The life of what-might-yet-be from the grave
Of soulless conformity, but though your words
Nest in my ears like the hallelujahs of birds,

Canto 3

They spread their wings on fantasy that preserves
The past even as it lifts up your speech
To a place neither of us on our own could reach

Where time lost becomes the power to teach."
"Patrick," she said, "we're both one and not-one,
For included in friendship's celebration

Is the power of self-annihilation—
Without that surrender contraries would die,
The progression of thought would quickly run awry,

And the only word we'd share would be goodbye.
Here in this place you became a kind of priest
Hearing others' confessions and not least

The silent roar of that intimate beast
That in the shadow of human life conspires,
Condemned to loneliness by a world that requires,

As Blake said, *binding with briars my joys & desires*,
But your mental transsubstantiation
Transformed monsters into angels—the creation

Of love's body, not a mystification,
But the being beyond the self-inflicted pains
That burn the soul 'til only ashes remain

And love itself becomes a ball and chain.
Born from the ashes of finite coverings,
A bridge built over infernos of suffering,

Paradise is infinite recovering.
Sometimes to this place your past lovers came by
And I saw the gaze of affection in your eye

As you served and tended them without a sigh,
And though your love for them had long since cooled—
You'd found the one whose heart over yours ruled—

Comedy, Book Three

Nothing in your gracious service could occlude
The tenderness that never died but transformed
Into a subtle flame that gently warmed

The space between you and these souls who swarmed
Toward the rays that unselfconsciously beamed
From your heart and awakened in theirs what might have seemed

Like a beacon to those lost at sea, which redeemed
Them by turning on a light in their memory,
And this was your special gift, a rarity

Among men that arose from the clarity
Of your amorous mind that swore a fealty
To all the traces of love as the passionate wake

Of an unnamable truth you'd never forsake
Because love is thought that forges a key
To unlock the door behind which the mystery

Is unraveled of desire's common destiny."
"You made me seem better than I could've been,"
I said, "when you spoke like this to me back then,

But not loving I thought a political sin,
For every woman I'd ever loved became
A step toward a paradise regained."

She answered, "A feeling you've never profaned
And now would call it minimal communism,
A word that seemed only to create a schism

Back then, but like someone on a mission
You never surrendered the truth you saw in the word,
Despite false prophets who wanted it interred

And dogmatists who made the concept absurd
By divorcing it from the love of multitude
And making the state into its substitute

Canto 3

With laws that try to suppress the absolute
Truth, which no finite law or rule can express
Because the truth is always in excess

And appears only as limitless progress
Toward a goal we can only imagine."
Then I replied, "At first like a contagion,

I walked in here and you could see the rage in
Me that hid the mourning for all love lost
I foolishly thought would be my permanent cross

Until your wit and grace provided a gloss
That made me see my self-willed stupidity,
Though you spoke with kindness and lucidity

And saw in my elective affinities,
Including my errors, a progression,
Absolute in itself, that taught this lesson—

Love of truth is the only real heaven
Because it annihilates the covers that block
The infinite within minds interlocked

From which arises a power that can rock
The universe and awaken the multitude
To its own divinity that must include

Every finite part of the human brood.
The multitude's essence is cooperation
And evil is the act of negation

That seeks to limit the power of creation
To acts that give rise to the wealth of nations.
Love is the first step toward liberation

When the heart is given without reservation."

CANTO 4

Suddenly Pat looked up toward the door behind me,
So naturally I turned around to see
And inside the door next to the bar a black

Man stood whose presence did nothing to distract
The spirits there, since back in my younger days
Such a man, if he chose to enter the place,

Would have been treated with democratic grace,
And if some hadn't Pat would've shown them the door.
But most black folk wouldn't have put much store

In a statement like that since it didn't accord
With their experience of life in the South.
But as I saw the man looking about,

I heard these words come out of Pat Smith's mouth:
"Richard Wright! Come meet the man who summoned
You here for things you two have in common,

Though in all likelihood you've already cottoned
Onto the place you occupy in his head,
But at least in that place neither of us is dead

Because our lives have become thoughts that have bred
Other thoughts that form an infinite series
And become something more than endless theories

But lift up mental warriors like valkyries
And incorporate them into truth's permanent
Revolution, a force always immanent,

Always now, and by touching the infinite—
As you did when you wrote things that were true
And transformed experience that made you blue

Into action that turned another screw
To force the absolute to show its face
And become for the multitude a saving grace—

Canto 4

You touched the universal that had to embrace
    Everyone, even those of a different race."
As she spoke, Richard Wright came to our table

And said, "Time has made the world more able
    To accommodate people who look like me,
    Despite the resurgence of racist hostility

And the new fantasy of replacement theory,
    But in my tour of this man's archive I found
Conditions of what may be our common ground—"

Pat interrupted, "Richard, please sit down,"
    Which he promptly did, then said, "Identification
    Has become all the rage in this broken nation,

And identities can challenge that old caucasian
    Dominance when others want their inclusion in
    The universal, at least that's where they begin,

But disappointment can cause their heads to spin
    And infinite truth surrenders to finitude
    That makes a mockery of multitude

With walls between and within nations that exclude
Each group from the others until the words 'brothers'
    And 'sisters' become alibis that hide ruptures,

    Turning multitude into a sea of vultures.
But you"—he looked at me—"somehow transgressed
    White identity when to you my life expressed

    Being that incorporated all the rest.
    Small synchronicities taught you a lesson
When you learned we were both sons of a Nathan

    And for both of us paternal alienation
    Shaped our destinies that intersected first
In Memphis where childhood felt like a curse,

Comedy, Book Three

But elsewhere I'd already done my worst
When at three I set fire to my grandma's house
(Just as you once crawled like a mischievous mouse

Into a dirty clothes cabinet whereabouts
You played with matches on your Mom's laundry,
And it remains to you quite a quandary

How you burned some things and got away scott free).
Then later, living in that river city,
I found a friend like you Irish American,

Since the white guys who called me 'nigger' called him
A 'pope lover' (and 'mackerel snapper'
Was the name you got called by local crackers)

And though not the same he still became my backer,
And his card got me books from the old Cossitt
Library down by the river, which wasn't legit

Of me but the only way I could outwit
The racist mandate that said 'Stay ignorant.'
But later you had your own predicament

When you made a choice that was not so innocent,
Because you worked in the same place but not in
The same building (after they committed the sin

Of replacing a castle with something more akin
To a box) and in non-circulating stacks
Where all the old books go to die in packs

You found brand-new editions on the racks
By Rosa Luxemburg—put there to hide
Them from curious eyes that one day might decide

To find out for themselves what lies inside
These volumes written by a notorious red.
Someone thought they were better dead than read,

Canto 4

But you thought to liberate them instead
And give back to the people what belonged
To the people, which to you didn't seem wrong,

And the same for me, we both had gone beyond
The identities society had assigned
To us, and found ourselves no longer inclined

To submit to categories predefined.
Similarly we both bent toward communism,
Because we saw in it common wisdom,

But soon felt trapped by narrow dogmatism,
So communists contra communists we became
And my friend Ralph Ellison did much the same,

Which may be why his New York fiction remains
For you a version of your own history.
You worked in hospitals as an orderly,

At the Post Office, at Boy's Clubs, just like me.
Chicago and New York meant liberty
To us both but then we came to realize

The dream of escape to the North was based on a lie.
These overlaps in our lives would seem trivial
To some but accidental material

Can become the condition of something spiritual
When it forces us to see the common,
The generic being that we all become

When we recognize ourselves in everyone."
Then I had something to say, "I never knew
The hunger or terror that came to you

From people who look like me, but this is true—
I always felt outside, different, alone,
And though all literature was my comfort zone,

Comedy, Book Three

Black Boy and *Invisible Man* gave me a home
In imagination, an identification
That promised a different kind of nation

And pinpointed a different destination
For communist desire—not dictatorship
Of any class or party as the whip

To keep multitude firmly in its grip—
But identification with the universal
And knowledge that the thing deemed most personal,

The false covering we call individual,
Is the outward expression of generic truth,
And like the singularity of the blues

It harbors infinities that won't exclude
Anyone from the only paradise
That can be projected by human eyes.

James Joyce in *Ulysses* saw through the disguise
Of minute particulars whose finite being
Has the power to express infinite being,

The essence behind the appearance of human being.
Finite intersections of the lives of others
With our own can become material conductors

That guide us to the place where all ruptures
Become the conditions of new identities
That incorporate individualities

Into undivided commonality.
In reading your life I felt my own to such
A degree that our two infinities touched

In the common dream to make a world more just."

CANTO 5

Then Phyllis came up to our table and said,
"There's a curious thing about being dead,
You happily go where angels fear to tread,

Places in life that once inspired your dread,
Like spending time in the company of fame
That makes you feel how much you're not the same,

Because in the end so many knew your name,
Richard, while friends and lovers alone knew mine—
But in death the light of a different truth can shine

That forces differences to realign
Where no one is up or down, in or out,
And equality is no longer in doubt—

Where spirits don't have the motive to flout
One another as singularities flow
Into a common stream and become nouveau

Through intersections with others that force a tableau
Of identities that might have been but were not
Because truth was buried under the rot

Of blind submission to lies that became the lot
Of too many who turned away and forgot
The love that once moved them to embrace others.

Love's an x-ray that penetrates covers
That bind and keep us closed like unread books.
This one used to read me in a way that shook

Me up because I could not bear the look
That reflected something in me I thought I'd lost
And feared its resurrection would be a cross,

A passion for which I feared too high a cost.
I walked away from him and other friends,
Then tried to love other men but the ends

Comedy, Book Three

Were violent and I felt that love condemns
One to a prisonhouse of abjection,
Though one man loved me and offered his protection

Like a father after the real one's defection,
But I feared it was another form of subjection.
In time I came to see who the enemy

Was, the one who threatened my autonomy,
And discovered it was none other than me.
The whole love thing finally just made me laugh,

Maybe not the last one but a laughter that lasts,
And like John Lennon I looked back on loves past
And knew I loved them all, men and women,

And their tenderness broke me out of prison
Even when I didn't know I was free."
"Sister," Wright said, "we make a community

With the living and the dead, not a unity
Or a fusion but a communion of differences,
Singularities that force us to know what is

Beyond what the world counts as existences.
James Baldwin said, 'Nobody knows my name,'
But the blues isn't about assigning blame—

No, it's about blasting through borders that frame
What we see, forcing into visibility
All human forms and the multiplicity

Of being that refuses immobility
For infinite becoming, the absolute,
Which is not a finite statement of truth,

Or a law the state says is beyond dispute,
But like Heraclitus' river, it stays
The same by changing—truth constantly strays

Canto 5

    Because it lives by carving new pathways
Through inert wastelands of dead ideas, dogmas
That cover the way forward like frozen magma—

    The absolute is the infinite panorama
    Imagination alone has the power to see,
    The direction of human possibilities,

    And its weapon is the positive energy
    Of love that regenerates the frozen hearts
Of those who have lost sight of the infinite part,

The creative power of thought to send out sparks
That set the world aflame with passionate dreams
    Like windows on a scene beyond what seems.

    Sister, you were like a magnet to those streams
      Of human desires that seek to go higher,
      You captured their lights like a magnifier

      To force a ray of intellectual fire
      That burned away the mental cataracts
    That keep most people blindly on the tracks

    Of social conventions that cause them to react
      But never out of wild desire to act
From the love of others, and others know your name,

    Sister, and after you, were never the same,
    Because you can't measure a life by fame,
And like this one's mother you sent forth beams

    That shed a light on all the false regimes
    That claim ownership of truth like a thing
That can be bought and sold, but you would sing

A different song and your voice became a spring
That gave birth to a river that swelled and flowed
    Into more lives than you could have been told

Comedy, Book Three

While you lived, but for someone like you who breaks the mould
There's something greater than fame—let's call it soul,
That's what you had in abundance and shared with all—

Everyone you touched heard and answered your call."
Then she said, "What about the times I was unkind?"
I answered, "Because you have a critical mind,

At times to others' feelings you were blind,
But flaws in a diamond make it more unique,
And none of us back then could escape critique,

And our common affections could be oblique.
But when I finally met the love of my life,
I remembered D. H. Lawrence and realized

How one woman can incorporate the lives
Of all women, and how when you love someone
All the feelings from your past loves become

Fused with what you love in the one who has won
Your heart—every lover is a teacher,
And through each passion we struggle to reach her,

The one who gives direction to our future,
But to everyone we've ever loved we owe
The gift because the image of each one sowed

The dream in our hearts that kept us on the road,
And even if that road comes to an end
Before we come to that most blessèd friend,

Nothing's lost, no sign can evil portend,
Because the road itself is paradise,
And the passionate depths of a lover's eyes

Are visions of eternity undisguised."
Richard then laughed and said, "You're a dreamer,
Who lives in a fallen world full of schemers,

Canto 5

But experienced dreamers can be redeemers—
From Jesus to Blake to Martin Luther King,
They give us visions of hope that all our dreams

Can be reforged into a wedding ring
That binds our heavens and hells in a marriage
With the power to force realities deemed savage

To bend toward the goal they would disparage.
My Memphis hell became the ladder I climbed
Into a world where my intellect shined

And transformed catastrophe into sublime
Self-expression, like the blues a celebration
Of life that depicted the truth of our nation

And planted its seed in multiple generations.
I made my share of mistakes, committed sins,
And like a fool fell for that monster Stalin,

But the lessons I took from the times I had fallen
Only strengthened my will never to surrender
To injustice, never to lose sight of splendor

That may lie buried under wastes that render
It invisible to the multitude, but to keep
The fires burning while brothers and sisters sleep

Is the task of the artist time cannot defeat."
Then Pat Smith decided to conclude this round:
"This one had to fight his way out of this town,

But it lives on in the memories that rebound
Through his imagination, but now he must
Move on, and in his own vision place his trust.

Falling or rising, his life won't be a bust."

CANTO 6

"Every honest book is a revelation
That addresses a future beyond the fate of nations,
But now I hear the call of emanations

Who give to my words their own innovations—
To each of them I owe a visitation—
Think of it as my dissemination,

A fancy word for thought's self-generation."
Thus spoke Richard Wright before he left us,
But at his exit I looked on breathless,

Until Pat said, "Are dreamers so fleshless
That they go on without food, drink, or sleep."
I answered, "Imaginary time can sweep

You through infinities beyond the heap
Of temporal waste through which we daily trudge
In lives that sometimes feel like endless drudge,

Which leads some to resent, hate, and begrudge
Others when like Sisyphus they feel judged
By some unwritten law, but imagination

Has the power to conquer time with inspiration
That conveys eternity in a microsecond,
Which leaves the body refreshened, not weakened,

And a life that felt like death becomes quickened.
Dante's dream did not scorn the rule of time
Because only heaven could be sublime

And everything below must be assigned
Finite duration, but I see no division
Between heaven and earth because the one

Embraces the other as its inner condition
Like lovers who transform physical finitude
Into the temporal fire of beatitude,

Canto 6

An event whose immeasurable magnitude
Is time redeemed, which teaches us that flesh
Is spirit, spirit flesh, nothing can repress."

"What you mean," Pat said, "I can only guess—
You always tried to say things unsayable—
But I take it you mean everyone's capable

Of touching the absolute that's unnamable
Because its manifold names are uncountable
And what's not-one can never have one name.

But come back to earth, it would be a shame
If you took your abstractions for the whole game."
Then Phyllis announced, "It's time to hit the road,

And I'd love to follow you and share the load—
For the heavy weight of truth won't let you go
And isolation stalks upon the way—

But in your memories this is where I stay.
Still isolation doesn't mean you're alone—
Those who love freely, even when they roam,

Carry inside everyone whose light has shone
On them, a multitude that becomes their home."
In that instant The Last Laugh was consumed

By a white light that filled me with warmth, not doom,
While my mental being felt like a vast room
And in it all my friends and lovers reside,

For together we form a constellation that bides
Through all the setbacks and losses of time,
And this told me, nothing is left behind,

Everything loved must eternally shine
And darkness is the shadow true life casts.
Then the light gradually faded until at last

Comedy, Book Three

A place appeared to me from out of my past.
It was Cortlandt Alley where I first came
When I hitched to New York City with the aim

Of getting aboard Trotsky's symbolic train—
Destination permanent revolution.
Then I saw what I knew must be illusion,

The face of a man approaching whose intrusion
Threatened me with the memory of his vow.
Towering over me he said, "Only now

Do I catch up with you, though nothing foul
Could I intend, despite what I once said
In a drunken reverie after you'd been bled

Publicly in a mock trial by that gang of reds
(Most of whom are now—you might think—quite dead)
And though the bleeding may have been symbolic,

Dogmatic terrorism feels diabolic.
Back then Marxism-Leninism was my credo,
But living with me you could not fail to know

My faith in the revolution of libido,
And Stonewall meant something to me the Sparts
Didn't get because it wasn't in Marx,

But my desire followed multiple arcs
For men or women—and wasn't communism
Itself polymorphous, which led to schisms,

Each one accusing the other of revisions?
Yes, I fell for that line lock, stock, and barrel,
And failed to see how much the endless quarrel

Caused multitude's desire to unravel.
Differences constitute the world but intersections
Cut through multiplicities of the not-one

Canto 6

With the transformative love of the common,
    And that love is the communist heaven.
For a while I lived with you in the space of a dream,

    And we both saw ourselves projected on a screen,
        Midnight cowboys, who on each other leaned,
    And you saw yourself as Ratso and I was Joe,

But you were the innocent one who captured my soul
    Because your mind was free and gloried in its
    Autonomy, which I feared would be eclipsed

    As soon as Robertson got his first glimpse
        Of a power he would not allow to exist,
        For fear you might one day openly resist

    His unquestioned authority, but what I missed
        Was what he'd do to me, how he'd break me—
        His verbal pistol whipping would guarantee

    That all the young comrades would come to see
        Me as a contemptible worm, the true enemy
        Of the working class—slimy, gutless, stupid—

Well, that's how I felt by the time Robertson got rid
    Of me, because the choice was either crawl
    Or resign, and that's when I remembered all

    Our conversations, because somehow you saw
        What was coming, though it wasn't Nelson,
    As we both joked, who would be our own Stalin,

    Since we both knew Jim was the real problem.
You walked away and left me trapped in a prison,
        And in time I came to realize the reason

        I couldn't move was my own submission
        To a fantasy—reified words that became
        Weapons we used in a political game

Comedy, Book Three

Whose ultimate goal was to assign the blame
For the movement's failure to change anything.
We laughed at men like Martin Luther King,

Since we alone had the theory that would bring
Liberation to all who learn how to sing
To our tune as the chorus of our song,

But inside the org here's how things went so wrong.
Beware friendship! It might become a clique
And Marx forbid, people privately critique

The leadership because the smallest leak
Can cause the boat to sink, and criticism
Undermines democratic centralism,

And changing direction is opportunism,
If not the mortal sin of revisionism,
And believing in the multitude's wisdom

Only results in half-baked reformism.
So the revolution is a game of Follow-
The-Leader with militants who are hollow

Inside because whoever can't swallow
Dictates and lies from above will get thrown out.
So people like you and me are put to rout

And the movement becomes religion banning all doubt.
Two years after you were gone—I was gone
And Dave and others you admired had withdrawn.

In your gaze I see that for you I now belong
Among the dead, but the truth is—you don't know.
I am only a projection from long ago,

Like an image you once saw at a picture show."

CANTO 7

Looking at Nick, all I could feel was affection,
Remembering the time he gave me his protection,
But now I was the older since he looked young,

Just as he did when our friendship had begun.
So I said, "You once promised to hunt me down
If I left the organization that we both found

Like a ship whose drunk captain had run it aground,
But we thought it was only his dogmatism
That perverted our vision with astigmatism,

Though in time I saw beyond bureaucratism
To the flaw in theory that tries to substitute
Itself for the complex desire of multitude,

Whose whirlwinds cannot be contained by rude
Channels to force change without deviations,
Without wandering thought and diffuse action

That always runs the risk of reaction.
But when we make the movement a police state—
When only obedience becomes the way

To keep revolution from fading away—
We become the enemy that would betray
Ourselves and the multitude we claim to serve

And our true goal is simply to preserve
Our power over them when it is not
The will to protect our sect like a plant in a pot.

We lose connection with the earth and the lot
Of those whose roots should be intertwined with ours."
Then Nick answered: "You think I lived in a tower?

Like professors who while away the hours
Writing militant texts that have no effect,
Though some imagine themselves members elect

Comedy, Book Three

Of the avant-garde who think they can direct
The world from above with words like Rapunzel's hair
   That others may climb up and breathe the air

Of their pure reason with which they write a prayer
   To a future that never comes because without
   Action and results all they can sow is doubt,

Which causes people to lose hope and drop out,
   As you did when you decided to go it alone
And imagined you could forgo a political home

   And make revolution by writing a poem."
Then I spoke: "Never alone, because in my head
The multitude lives, even those who are dead,

   And revolution's as common as bread
   If you look for its symptoms in everyday life—
Even commodities you would scorn can be rife

   With desires that concentrate a beam of light
   On the heart of multitude that slowly awakes
Through tremors that become silent earthquakes,

   Forcing change we can hardly see take place
   Because it enters our world with a quiet grace
Through songs, films, plays, stories, pictures, and dreams.

   Then some few look out one day and it all seems
   A new world, and they celebrate—but others,
Seeing the same thing, stop in their tracks and suffer

   A shock that fuels reaction and would smother
      The subtle fire of slow revolution
   For fear they'll lose the comfort of illusion,

And so forwards and backwards without conclusion
The process discreetly unfolds through minute steps,
   But in the balance despite retrograde checks

Canto 7

Progress is made toward a world that resets
　　The permanent revolution to begin
　　Again, since infinite progress has no end—

But thought cannot be words alone or transcend
　　The necessity of action, though it must be
　　Multiform, without guardrails to guarantee

A goal pre-ordained by any theory."
Then Nick: "Perhaps we are not so far apart
　　In believing revolution must have a heart

But you need to confront the antithesis of your art—
　　He's upstairs in the grey green space that survives
　　In memory, the office where you once arrived,

Penniless but bold with the will to sacrifice
　　Your time and labor to a course militant,
　　Though revolutionary itinerant

Might best describe your wayward predicament."
He guided me toward the building's entrance where
　　On the elevator I breathed dust-laden air,

Which evoked the memory of the doctrinaire
　　Atmosphere in the dull light of that bureau
　　I had once entered and was about to go

Through again, this time an imaginary show.
Nick knocked on the grey door, then through the peephole
　　A shadow covered the pin of light like a soul

Cloaked in darkness that had taken its toll
　　And left the man nothing to play but the role
　　Of negation as warden of the prisonhouse.

Then the door opened to a voice that had no doubts:
　　"Can't death spare me reactionist factionists
　　Who dared to think they could be anatomists

Comedy, Book Three

Of my leadership, somehow always in crisis—
The sad fate of the true revolutionist—
But I suppose the etiquette of the dead,

Or whatever rule operates in this man's head,
Grants you entry to my memorial space."
As we entered the room, I felt the absence of grace,

Enshrined in the man's cold calculating face.
As he reached his desk, he grabbed a jeroboam
Of cheap red wine, saying he drank alone

And never would share any with anyone.
After three or four glasses, he looked at us
And said, "No words can express my total disgust

With the likes of scum like you I could never trust.
The revolution requires iron discipline,
Which is also the test to see who is genuine,

But this one, Nick, lacked the stamina for submission,
Which I told you but you wouldn't listen
And let this traitor to his class infect

You with his virus until you chose to reject
The lines I dictated, always correct,
But in the end so many parasites—

Even the one I dared to call my wife—
Infiltrated until expulsions were rife,
And when I was finally expelled from life,

I came here to my own true paradise,
Where the only person I have to convince is me,
As I live the dream of absolute purity,

The only true avatar of Trotsky."
Then Jim Robertson reached for the bottle and downed
Two more glasses of wine, while Nick frowned

Canto 7

And said, "I used to think you were profound
With phrases like 'deformed workers state'
For the Soviet Union, and we had no debate

About Mao's apothegms being half-baked
Formulas only designed to indoctrinate
The masses on the necessity to hate

Rather than to inform and educate
Them on how to practice worker's autonomy,
But your own practice was mental lobotomy

Driven by your own paranoid dichotomy
Between the correct line and truth as process,
Because you don't transform minds through duress

That produces the false harmony of the hopeless
And substitutes for positive creation
Endless scissions through the rule of negation

That condemns real thought as a deviation,
And lets fusion kill cooperation,
Which must be the essence of communism."

"So you chose the path of factionalism,"
Jim retorted, "Was that the act of a comrade?"
And Nick: "Some of us thought you had gone mad

When you seemed to institute rules that forbade
Friendship without authorization from you,
Or required pre-clearance to think something was true,

Or made loyalty to Jim the only glue
That could keep us bound together on the road
To the revolution by you alone foretold—

A commodity like snake oil that you sold."

CANTO 8

As Jim drained another glass of red wine,
I thought perhaps it was booze that made him malign,
But he said, "Idiot! I'm in your head and know

Your thoughts, but I told you long, long ago
About my overactive adrenal glands
And how wine helps me keep a steady hand,

So don't compare me to your average man."
All I could say was, "I don't give a damn
How much you drink, but what you did to my friend

And others whose power of thought you condemned
Because to your will it refused to bend—
All that did was contract the scope of thought,

Which must be universal and free, not fraught
With false logic driven more by terror
Than the quest for truth that can redeem the error

It generates by making the standard-bearer
Not one man or dogma but the common—
The essence of truth itself as the not-one,

A property that resides in everyone."
Jim laughed, "What a lot of abstract nonsense!
Truth generates error? What was my offense

If truth itself is only a pretense?
You're just spouting more bourgeois relativism."
"What's more bourgeois than autocratic wisdom,"

I replied, "that congeals thought into a frozen dictum,
Like a dam that converts wild rivers into lakes
And allows only enough flow to escape

That can electrify a finite space
By forgetting the infinity of the race
Toward a future beyond temporal measure.

Canto 8

But the dam one day must break under pressure
Because the force of a truth cannot be stopped
And everything that blocks it will be knocked

Down by the internal power unlocked
Behind the finite wall meant to contain it,
And all the negations you use to name it—

Proletarian or bourgeois—only frame it
In a way to cause positive truth to break through."
"So you're one of those," he said, "who twist the screw

Backwards, a revisionist who would eschew
Necessary violence against the class
That will never surrender power without a last

Stand, ready to incite the fascist mass
It holds in its hand like a cocked gun that's aimed
At the heart of the Prometheus enchained,

The workers of the world who can't be restrained
By pacifist cowards too paralyzed to act."
The accusation stung because I lacked

Righteousness that might have answered his attack
In kind, so I said, "You're not entirely wrong,
But I refuse to sing the same old song,

Not with you, Lenin, Trotsky, or Mao Zedong—
Whom, by the way, you always claimed to shun,
But your nuclear political fission has done

Enough damage to make you Mao's son
With power not out of the barrel of a gun
But out of isolation from those who doubt

The dogma you promoted from your redoubt,
That comic-book fortress of solitude
That time shrank down to nothing but a rude

Comedy, Book Three

Hovel so peripheral to multitude,
It's like a floater on collective vision.
The word 'bourgeois' to me lacks some precision—

A word on the left that always connotes derision
But then gets used for any who disagree
With those who proclaim their Marxist authority,

Which has inspired more than one murder spree—
So I just call it 'wealth' that forms a block
Against the multitude from fear of the shock

To the world should the people's minds interlock
Into a common thought of their own power
To create a world where equality can flower

And value is not measured by the hour.
Capitalists personify capital or wealth,
Wrote Marx, but must we assume that bourgeois stealth,

Compelling the destruction of everyone else,
Is the essence of their being, which would justify
Their annihilation—and soon wouldn't we apply

The same penalty to any who question why
Revolution means so many must die?
History teaches that this has already happened,

And in the eyes of the world it has blackened
The word 'communism,' which has come to mean
A system or state that transforms into a machine

The multitude in ways that were unforeseen
By Marx, for whom the word expressed the idea
Of a world where property would not be the

Sole human value, and he could foresee the
Possibility that humankind would transcend
Class through struggle, but how that fight would end

Canto 8

In stateless communism or exactly when
That would come to be, he left to posterity,
And he knew the consciousness of the bourgeoisie

Was dominated by ideology
That made them into things, parts of the machine
Of capital, but what remained unseen

Was how from capital logic would supervene
A popular consciousness that would colonize
The vanguard class that Marx mythologized,

Until from capitalism itself would arise
The multitude, which, though it contains everyone,
Produces class struggles through the scissions

Of those who fear forms of coalition
Without an exclusion clause to protect their finite
Identity, and in that way lose sight

Of the common and forget no struggle's right
Unless it includes everyone in the fight.
Fusion is a form of separation,

Because it requires identification,
Often with one man and the fantasy of nation,
But in the end its essence is negation,

The antithesis of cooperation
That defeats the one through the power of not-one.
That's multitude itself, individuals,

Beyond categories, all originals.
Communism is the multitude's movement—
Whose goal, Marx wrote, is 'the free development

Of individualities,' which meant
A power that lies below and rises above
The state, fueled not by hate or revenge but love,

Comedy, Book Three

Though you could describe militant love as tough
Because its faith in people never dies,
No matter how many times they succumb to lies,

No matter how many times they fail to rise
Up against injustice—for to theorize
May serve the truth but can't monopolize

Its process that may take a turn and surprise
The revolutionaries who must catch up
With unforseen movements that disrupt

Their expectations and cause them to reconstruct
Their thought, but never to think they can conduct
The masses from above like some vanguard

That takes the authority to crack down hard
Should any section of multitude deviate
From a predetermined goal or conciliate

With class enemies rather than gravitate
Toward the overthrow of the bourgeois state.
Permanent revolution requires patience

And persuasion committed to truth, but not violence,
Which can only bring to power damaged souls.
Though it may be justified when used to oppose

A fascist state with homicidal goals,
It can never pave the way to communism,
Which can never be equated with statism,

Because every state produces a schism
Between those who look up and those who look down,
And the state can only govern finite ground,

Not the infinite future that has no bounds.
Revolution is not evolution—
Nothing will change without the resolution

Canto 8

To act, but the goal is not retribution,
And terror is counterrevolution
Because it imprisons the communist idea

And makes dogma into a panacea."
Jim stared into his wine and said nothing,
Then looked at me indifferently like a king

And said, "Excuse me, did you say something?"

CANTO 9

Nick put his hand on my shoulder and said,
"We're wasting our time here, for this one is dead,
Not only in body, but the spirit's been bled

Until even the symbolic color red
Betrays its own meaning for a false paradise
That hides behind the white wall of his eyes

And to his own intellect wears a disguise.
Because he played a role in our history,
He assumes the image of living memory,

But to the world at large his dull legacy's
Only a footnote to a forgotten sect."
Soon we left the building and went direct

To Canal Street where I had to recollect
The place I'd known but mixed with sights and sounds,
Artificial memories with a beat that pounds

Into the brain history's nightmare but confounds
The horror with a strange beauty, so I spoke:
"Nick, you once took me as a kind of joke

To Little Italy where I mispoke—
Loudly in a restaurant—about gangsters,
But you told me this was no place for pranksters,

And lest we should awaken some blank stares,
We needed to take precautions not to displease.
That place came back to me in Scorsese's

Cinema and the way it dissected the disease
Money injects into our lives like a drug
That makes us all blind to the hole we've dug

Ourselves into, and the way we unplug
Our brains from the intellectual commonwealth
Where we actually enhance the being of self

Canto 9

Through annihilation of being only oneself,
What William Blake called a mind-forged manacle
That releases a force of cruelty tyrannical

That rules us until we become cannibals
Of the spirit, swearing fealty to a gang
That seduces us with the illusion of swank

Existence through the gift of superior rank
If only we become contract killers
Who take out not just bodies but the pillars

Of human hope, the dream of becoming builders
Of a world where the hall of Justice isn't a dream,
Where we don't have to submit to a mindless machine,

Where the streets of America don't have to be mean.
Not far from here in Chinatown was a place
That once sheltered immigrants of a different race—

Call it the not-white—which some said debased
The monochrome vision of America,
A blindness that derived from hysteria

Of those whose power and wealth made them wary of
The races that might become one without fusion
That would make an even more threatening intrusion

Into white power because it means inclusion
Of difference need not erase but enhance cultural
Identity, which becomes universal

Diversity, perhaps the true rehearsal
Of communism, not the proletariat's
Dictatorship that like Judas Iscariot

May give itself the kiss that would bury it
Through a party that claims to have married it.
Scorsese recreated Paradise Square

Comedy, Book Three

Where he lifted the veil on a history that laid bare
Violence that produced the alternative world of gangs—
Chinese, Blacks and the Irish bared their fangs

    To each other and against all the harangues
    Of their superiors—and there I began
    In some ancestor, the member of a band

That fled hunger and hate to come to this land,
Where they quickly learned freedom meant being white,
Which moved them to betray themselves and fight

    Any whose very existence challenged their right
    To turn their backs on children of the night.
So the Irish became white and thought they were free,

    But this kind of freedom was a poverty
    Of spirit that made their flesh a commodity,
    Bought and sold, while the multitude's power

Was sacrificed to wealth that would devour
The hope that drove so many across the seas."
As we reached Church Street, I looked to my left and was seized

    By the memory of the towers that had ceased
    To exist, long after I had worked across
From them, and I thought of Scorsese's expression of loss

    In a voice from the past that ponders history's cost:
    "For the rest of time, it would be like," he feared,
    "No one even knew we was ever here."

    All the voices of the gone pressed on my ear
    Like I used to hear them on my nightly sojourn
    As I left the Church Street Station where once burned

    The fire of a wildcat strike by those who affirmed
    Their autonomy, which meant they had unlearned
    Submission, and I bore that truth in the dark

Canto 9

As I wandered through streets toward Columbus Park,
Haunted by the ghosts of the old gangs of New York,
Whose names I only learned when revelations

On a movie screen showed me the birth of a nation.
Then Nick said, "I hear your thoughts and can see
Why you believe dreams are not just fantasy,

For their power can break through reality
That binds us to a fixed time and place
By forcing us to see beyond the waste,

The sediments of despair and loss of faith,
When the world becomes a finite prisonhouse
And the mind of multitude is clogged with doubts

While conservatives rise up to put to rout
The last vestiges of hope that only dreams
Can keep alive when those around us seem

Congealed into a million frozen screams.
The real becomes illusion when we forget
That time is a river that flows without regret

With infinite power that can reset
The future and that way keep hope alive."
As our walk through time continued it revived

A past present in which Stonewall survived,
Not just a gay bar off Seventh Avenue
Next to a little park where we used to

Spend time in the Village but something forever new,
An event that like a slow explosion blew
A new wind into the world that forced a truth

That became more than the celebration of youth
But released from the earth all the human flowers
Whose seeds had been buried away from showers

Comedy, Book Three

By those whose fear of difference made them cowards.
Nick spoke, "Like all the other events we missed
With our eyes fixated on the past while we dissed

The present, the future of which would not desist—
Stonewall without other movements might not
Have been, and women too would cast their lot

With the multitude that began to take its shot.
The Civil Rights Movement first showed the way,
But we could only see it as a delay

Of the revolution whose law we had to obey
When what mattered was not to turn away
From multiple streams that flowed into one river.

Now I see our task was not to deliver
People to a promised land of our design
But to hear their voices and help to align

Them toward a future they alone define.
We should only be the caregivers who bless
The inner life of multitude on its quest

To realize the power it has possessed
Since time's beginning, which it can manifest
Only through cooperation and action,

The goal of which is not domination
Of others through the conquest of a state
But to seek continually to recreate

The collective body and mind of our connate
Individualities, so that we can be
The higher power we have so longed to see,

A human form that touches eternity."

CANTO 10

From Christopher Street we walked to Union Square
Because once I had a revelation there
Wandering through a labyrinth of bookstores where

Such wealth of human voices made me aware
Of divine immanence, a vast human creation,
Not monopolized by a class or nation,

And I felt the seduction of my vocation
That gave meaning to my first realization
Of the power of books when as a boy I read

About mutinies and revolts, and heard the dead
Come alive and bestow on me a grace
That said, "Whatever path in life you embrace,

Don't fear failure or think your time a waste,
For thoughts in words live on in printed texts
And the minds of others echo the effects

To create a circle that widens and connects
Every singular event to the great archive—
Words, acts—nothing dies, everything survives,

And though we fall, a counterforce revives
The truth to which we sacrificed our lives."
Then I spoke, "Now the bookstores are mostly gone,

But they were once the promise of something beyond,
Which we couldn't see and many still don't see—
In hyperspace the archive's a vast sea

That becomes a counterpoint to the bourgeoisie
Who subject truth and art to the rule of money—
But the Web transgresses law to create a free

Zone with a network of roots like a god tree,
A living encyclopedia forever
Under revision as it transforms error

Comedy, Book Three

    Into a station on the road that's bearer
    Of a truth process that is never complete,
    And each detour comes back to us replete

With new directions that time won't deplete."
As we spoke we continued walking up Broadway
    To Fifth Avenue and then to where Fay Wray,

    Hapless heroine, was dragged to her dismay
    To the top of the Empire State Building by Kong,
    And once again I wanted to sing my song

About how in my dream the monster had dawned
    As the revelation of my own monstrosity,
    But I feared laughter at my grandiosity,

    When to my surprise Nick said, "Luminosity
Of the heart drove your monster out of the dark
Because you saw in the creature's fall a stark

Vision of a cruel history that in you sparked
    A will to rebellion before you even knew
    The realities from which that image drew,

    But a feeling that was inwardly true—grew
    Into your monster whose love of beauty
    Nurtured the desire for justice and the duty

    Of nonviolence as a force absolutely
    Committed—not to overthrowing the state
    But—to daily acts that would educate

The multitude on how to shift the weight
    Of power to themselves and collaborate
    Through mutual forgiveness to generate

The diffuse power of love and celebrate—
    Not the delusions of one man or nation—
But the untapped wealth of human cooperation

Canto 10

That produces the surplus of liberation."
Then I answered, "I wonder if what I hear
From you is my own voice echoed in my ear."

"Your continuing doubt," he said, "expresses fear
That death cancels every thought and emotion
And the meaning of time is loss through slow corrosion

Of memories reflecting love and devotion
To the not-me, but the self is not a thing
With a voice that from a singular source could spring,

But a wide river whose tributaries bring
Such fullness to the flood that may alter
A straight course and change the shape of water

To break through banks to spaces unchartered.
In itself the I is other, a multitude,
As Rimbaud surmised, a shared being imbued

With powers from history's infinite wake accrued.
I am he, you are he me we, all together,
Like John Lennon sang, in his great comether.

So don't keep doubting yourself about whether
You're of the egoist solipsist school—
Anyone who loves truth must become a fool

In the eyes of a world that can't see beyond the rule
Of static being that like a mask covers
The infinite becoming of the other,

The *potentia* in the heart of every lover."
Such dialogues continued until we came
To the great park where I thought he would remain

With me, but instead he said, "From this profane
Illumination I must now depart,
But if you follow your instincts through this park,

Comedy, Book Three

You will experience another arc
In your journey, from a person whose song echoed
Through your intellect with words that stilettoed

The heart of multitude on whom they bestowed
A neglected truth and gave it sublime resonance
In the common, our collective inheritance.

Goodbye, my friend, and if my life's desinence
Has been postponed, perhaps we'll meet again."
And instantly he was gone, but to what end

I didn't know but felt summoned by a wind
That drove me through the winding paths toward
The other side of the park where a green sward

Was set aside in memory of a lord
Of rock-and-roll, though his music was more than that,
An expansion of blues into a magnificat

Of the common dream that would burst with such éclat
Across the globe in a plain language that spoke
To all individuals, to every folk,

Calling out the dogmas that imprison hope
And betray the power of imagination
That can knock down the walls surrounding a nation

And all the lies that limit human creation.
I stood next to the concrete circle that framed
The word "IMAGINE" from the song that named

His life when he sought something more than fame.
In this imagined New York, there was no crowd,
Only a man sitting on a bench, head bowed,

But when he stood and removed a hood like a shroud,
I was confronted with John Lennon's smile.
"Now we've come together, let's walk a while,"

Canto 10

He said, and so we did for more than a mile,
Heading northeast back through the green dream
While I was captured by a voice that seemed

More alive than most of those the world has deemed
Celebrities, a name to cover a void.
"Fame," he said, "may have been the force that destroyed

Me, when the monstrous shadow it deployed
Covered me until I felt it would suffocate
The breath of imagination and shut the gates

Of my vision that meant to anticipate
A future where poetry is common to all,
And all human creatures sing and walk tall,

And creation raises you up without a fall.
Fame like a magnet attracts the hollow men
Who think you have the soul missing in them

When in truth you feel yourself dying within
And struggle just to survive and begin again.
I wasn't kidding when I sang I'm a loser—

Sometimes a clown and sometimes a boozer—
Because inside my self-love felt unsure
And if I began to think fame was the cure,

I learned such anesthesia won't endure
And the feelings you thought you'd killed come back with a vengeance,
Until fame felt like a prison sentence.

But I'm not here to confess and do repentance,
Only to express feelings I know you share,
Though from fame you may think yourself too much spared—

Trust me, you wouldn't want to sleep in that lair."

CANTO 11

I walked with John but thought there's something wrong,
Which made me want to talk about his song.
I said, "Your words taught me heaven could be

A negation of infinite possibility,
So the negation of a negation affirms
Our intellectual power that discerns

The real heaven that makes us more than worms,
Which is not a place but a process unyielding
Of imagination constantly building

On the dreams of multitudes always wielding
A power unconscious of itself that stirs
The common thought until an event occurs,

The momentous mental breakthrough that transfers
The mind's energy into singular acts,
Causing human freedom to expand or contract,

For there's no guarantee things won't go off track—
But if it does, it's time to begin again,
Against infinite truth failure is no sin,

Every detour shows another way in,
Though sometimes you can't tell heaven from hell."
But John's silence spoke like a metallic knell,

Echoing through park alleys and casting a spell
With memories of the bullet that disdained
His life and the creative power it contained—

And perhaps he wondered what might have remained
Of the legacy cut short by meaningless death.
Then he said, "I do not mourn the things that were left

Undone, nor want revenge for the mindless theft
Of a life too blessed for me to feel bereft
Now that I know the essence of me lives on

Canto 11

    And not in some dull fanciful place beyond
        Human experience but in the concrete
        Being of other minds infinitely replete

  With awareness that expands and never retreats
From the truths my simple words sometimes approached.
    But the future I lost gives me power to broach

    A tragic future that may come to encroach
      On truth processes with a will to negate
        Imagination's power to create

    A world in motion against one that stagnates
      Until it becomes a quagmire of mental rot,
      Zombie ideas that live in brains like bots

To insure the control of multitude by despots."
  We came to what should have been Fifth Avenue
    But instead faced a cold fog of ashen hue,

Thick and obscure, which John beckoned me through,
    Saying, "On the other side lies a future
      In which the state becomes a social tumor,

    While people regard truth as merely rumor,
      And think cruelty the essence of virtue."
We passed through the fog to a world that seemed averse to

    Sunlight, and gazing across the avenue,
      I saw a group of women in single file
  Marching with heads down and nary a smile,

  Followed by a man with a gun who seemed hostile,
    And he herded them toward the Guggenheim,
    Which I could not imagine the scene of a crime,

  But then with shock I read these words on a sign:
    "Guggenheim Women's Re-Education Unit"
      And below a motto expressing a tenet:

Comedy, Book Three

"What God creates art desecrates when it
Innovates and refuses to submit
To the holy truth of divine revelation"—

Attributed to the leader of the nation,
Ron Santissimo—so for answer I looked to John
Who said, "America in the name of Ron

Betrays itself in one future that's won
After the great liar who came before
Swindled the masses and opened the door

To the autocratic dream long held in store
By democracy's antithesis, a fragment
Driven by self-negation against attachment

To the infinite whole—those who fear the enjambment
Of differences, erasing their finitude,
Which defines their suffering as holy rectitude,

The sign of their election above the rude
Souls who dream of living as one multitude.
When I sang that the concept of God measures our pain,

I should have added art is how we regain
The paradises lost by the failure to see
All of humankind as the divine family,

Whose political essence is democracy.
For Santissimo women are the enemy—
Along with art, for both seek autonomy—

But listen to the words of his homily."
Then speakers throughout the city I heard broadcast
This speech: "I'm Ron Santissimo, your last

And most lasting leader speaking of the past
And the present, since I became your president
Forever, and replaced all the precedents,

Canto 11

    Like the Constitution, with a new testament,
For I speak with a voice that channels Jesus Christ,
    And therefore the things I say cannot be lies

    However far away they may seem to lie
    From empirical observation—just don't try
    To question my authority, or you'll pay

    A price, since the law now forbids you to say
      It's natural for people to be gay
Or for boys and girls to change into girls and boys,

    Or for people to choose the sexual joys
    They prefer, forgetting their duty to defer
    To God's authority—and I won't demur,

That means me, since the Holy Entrepreneur
    Chose me to be his sales representative
    To spread the new gospel of competitive

    Capitalism as a sacred imperative.
    First he created those in his masculine
    Image, and secondarily magdalenes

(Let them repent for having brought scandal in-
To the world!) who must be the handmaids of men
    In order to redeem their original sin—

    And to prevent their repeating it again,
    I've remade the legal system to force them
    To give birth, since at conception life begins.

    But life generates life some would contend,
    Never to end or begin again, which offends
    God who alone can cut that Gordian knot

And I'm the knife he uses to cut through the rot
    Of rational thought, which is why I've put a stop
To the speech and books of those who claim they're Woke,

Comedy, Book Three

And we've got prisons for those who think I'm a joke
And for women who reject God's natural yoke.
But to show we're willing to save a few sinners,

We send them to re-education centers,
Which some say is communism of the right
But I say wokism is communism, a blight

That murders the sleep of those who are upright,
And I'm not just talking about the night.
General sleep should enshroud the multitude

Always, for fear being awake will preclude
People's happiness by forcing them to think,
And before you know it they're addicted to drink

Or dope—or worse, going to see a shrink,
Which means self-knowledge that leads to insomnia,
Or everyone singing their own aria

Without harmony, which brings back the era of
Anarchy, the horrible nineteen sixties,
When the kids became either Marxists or gypsies—

Better to sleep than become a singing hippie,
Like Dylan or Lennon or Young or even the Boss.
God bless Reagan for trying to get across

'Born in the U.S.A,' but Springsteen lost
When he maligned our greatest anointed one.
Then the Stones attacked my John the Baptist for fun

Just because of the web of lies he'd spun,
But lies can be truthful if God so wills
And may be more conducive to sleep than pills

And putting the nation to sleep finally fulfills
The goal of my party and Divine Providence,
The truth of which hardly requires evidence,

Canto 11

And we need not invoke legal precedents
When we submit ourselves to the higher law.
Suspending the Constitution was our call

To save us from democracy's cabal."

CANTO 12

The speech went on and on like a boring song
Until I saw something else going on,
A band of men and women armed to the teeth,

Waving red banners that defied belief
With the words "Jesus Militia" in bold letters
Printed on them, and some few in fetters

Between the lines marched like breathless specters
Whose expressionless faces said hope is lost,
And leading this parade, bearing a cross

And a machine gun that said she was boss,
Was a woman who raised the gun to pause
The march and shouted in a tone most curt

While looking at me: "I am Lauren Blowdert,
Leader of these fighters for Jesus Christ,
And we punish all those who promote the lies

That God's son chose to forgive, not to chastise
His enemies, that he did not want vengeance,
Which would make him a pussy whose forbearance

Sets a poor example for his chosen descendants,
Namely those who are truly in his image,
For not everyone has divine peerage—

In the passage to heaven some belong in steerage.
But if you don't swear allegiance to Jesus
Right now my gang will beat the bejesus

Out of you, since only force will redeem us,
As women have learned who disrespected a fetus.
Redemption out of the barrel of a gun

Is the will of the father who governs everyone—
And can I help it if it's also a lot of fun?
The most holy Ron has enshrined this truth in law

Canto 12

And if necessary he'll kill you all,
With me the instrument at his beck and call.
You don't want to share the fate of our prisoners,

Secularist monsters who call themselves professors,
Now sentenced for the crime of indoctrination,
Teaching ideas that are an aberration

From the Christian laws of our gun-toting nation.
Now join us or by god I will see red."
I turned to John who said, "Because I'm dead

She can't see or hear me, but don't be misled,
Your dream is like the matrix, even this dream
Within a dream that may make reality seem

Fixed and immovable, but like a screen
That covers the eyes of the mind whether they're awake
Or asleep, this imaginary can operate

On mental vision with a will to negate
Imagination, for they are not the same.
The latter has the power to break the chain

That keeps thought bound within the finite frame
Of ideology, another name
For the imaginary, with which this future

Would kill the dream of democracy through a suture
Of the eyes to a spectral simulacrum
Of reality that refuses to make room

For infinity that threatens this poltroon
Who thinks she's made in God's image when in fact
She's forced the concept of God onto the rack

And tortured it until it bears the lack
Of spirit that constitutes her clotted brain.
To her, God is just as bigoted and insane

Comedy, Book Three

As herself, a kind of feminine John Wayne,
But the concept of God, if it means anything,
Should measure the joyous existence of everything,

The infinite variety of being
That incorporates all forms of sexual congress
And holds no form of love as something less,

If it is true, than absolute Godliness.
Now use your mental power to cast off
This deluded mob with empty heads who scoff

At the very idea of truth—and save these profs
Who may not know as much as they think but serve
The good whenever they manage to swerve

From the dull realm of opinions and follow the curve
Of thought that anticipates a future imperfect
In which the event only a few detect

Through their persistence can finally resurrect
The soul of multitude, which is divine."
My face must have conveyed to him some sign

Of my wonder at the event his words enshrined,
So he spoke again, "The answer's in your brain—
Jesus, Spinoza, Blake, and Marx, they name

The event that your life has struggled to reclaim
From the dead archives or the religious cult,
And I'm pleased to have lent my voice to the result.

Now take a stand against those who exult
In their ignorance and think sadism Christ-like."
Then Blowdert shouted, "Speak up, or we'll strike

Without hesitation because we're right
Since God's always on the side of religious might.
Join us and not only will you be saved

Canto 12

But you'll get a free AK, which real men crave."
Then I said, "How can I fear what doesn't exist?
I have to believe the multitude will resist

The future in which you live, so please desist
From this fantasy of what you will come to be—
You won't even be remembered by history.

So here and now take my valedictory."
That crew, without prisoners, vanished from the day
That showered the Guggenheim in solar rays,

Which restored to its architecture the praise
Of aesthetic vision, but John stood with me still
Because even in death he was more real

Than those so deaf they couldn't hear the peal
Of the knell that denounced their zombie ideas.
Then the prisoners chanted *esse est deus*

As one by one they took steps to leave us,
And I thought of music's power to free us.
"Well, I wouldn't have sung it in Latin,"

Said John. "Enough I had to learn Manhattan,
Just in time to be shot by an assassin.
But it seems that their chant must mean that everything

Is God, like that William Blake seemed to think,
Though at times I've imagined God must be extinct.
All I wanted was to write and sing my songs

And if my words could help to right some wrongs
Or make everybody feel they belong
To each other, that's my revolution.

But did my work become devolution,
The decline of my earlier evolution?
Sometimes I must admit I envied Paul

Comedy, Book Three

Whose success made my career feel like a fall
And I got carried away with our little brawl."
So I said, "Paul mostly obeyed the rules of pop

And that way to this day he's stayed on top,
But you gave something singular to rock,
Which came through your dissonance beyond pleasure,

Which popularity cannot measure,
And your raw and taut sensibility put pressure
On rock'n'roll with the force to expand its essence

Beyond the marriage and coalescence
Of folk, country, jazz, and the effluence
Of those who knew the meaning of being down,

Which despite your wealth and the way you played the clown
Was the hidden secret buried in your sound.
Above all else you were a man of the blues—

Even if the inner soul that was your muse
Sounded rubber or plastic to other crews,
You injected into it naked emotion

And expressed your love with tender devotion
And through a kind of lyrical explosion
Blasted away all the clichés of pop

With creative will that could only be stopped
By America's cruel unforgotten plot
To make the gun the voice of multitude,

Like a false prophecy with hatred imbued
That longs to put another corpse on a rood.
When you sang that they wanted to crucify you,

It wasn't sacrilege but just plain true."

CANTO 13

"God is a concept by which we measure our pain,"
John said, "and our joy, because they are the same,
When they come together in sunshine or rain,

Because in-between the rainbow sustains
The promise that better days to come remain.
In the darkest night you can imagine the light,

And the brightest day always leads back to night—
But whatever gets you through, man, is all right.
Now the time has come for you to take flight—

Like that Keanu Reeves soar up to a height
And meet another man's imagination,
Which will take you on a ride across the nation

To the next phases of your peregrination."
I looked up to see a large spheroid balloon
With a gondola that had plenty of room,

Then through effortless thought my body zoomed
Straight up faster than a bullet and reached the airship,
Though not to such a height as Keanu had skipped,

But enough to continue on my long strange trip.
After waving goodbye to John, around
I turned to face the crew with whom I was bound,

And one who seemed the leader approached to expound:
"We're the Chums of Chance and we live always on the go
In the creations of one whose books you know—

His name is Tom but you can call me Cosmo.
Now hang on and we'll soon be in Chicago.
The winds of imagination will get us there

Faster than Superman could fly through the air."
As if driven by a hurricane we flew,
Though nothing seemed to faze the comical crew,

Comedy, Book Three

And before I knew it Chicago came in view.
But my wonder made me ask, "Why must I stop
Here where a friend once gave me a place to flop

And where in a big hospital I got a job.
That friend still lives, and though we're not so close,
I'm still in awe of his life force that goes

On creating in his daughters living shows
Of the amorous heart that was his redemption,
With the loving wife who commands his full attention

As he celebrates all their self-inventions."
Then Cosmo explained, "There are some here whose names
You can't recall, and though it's not my aim

To pronounce on you a verdict that lays blame,
You learned a lesson here about the pain
That leaves on the social fabric a lasting stain,

An event from which you should never refrain
From remembering again, but now descend
This ladder, and since going down can end

Badly, which going up did not portend,
Please step slowly and carefully, my friend."
Down I climbed until I stood on Kimbark

Street next to where I once lived in Hyde Park.
Then a man approached who seemed about my age,
And he stopped in front of me as if to engage,

Saying, "You once awoke in me a rage,
Back when we both worked as hospital orderlies,
And you would always talk philosophically,

Which made you seem full of white pomposity
To your co-workers who were mostly black
Like me, but if your voice waxed too abstract,

Canto 13

You were still a member of our pack,
And we accepted you as one of us,
Until one day you made us question that trust

When we felt the edge of something unjust.
You announced off the cuff that you would soon leave,
And while that news didn't cause us to grieve,

The afterthought of your freedom bereaved
Us of ever feeling we'd have the like.
When someone asked, you said you would hitchhike

To California, which you took as your right,
But you didn't see it came from being white,
And then you couldn't grasp the reason why

Coldness and indifference was our goodbye.
For us Chicago was a home and a prison
Because the limit of what we could be was written

On our skin and all our hopes were slum-ridden,
Which meant they didn't inspire but caused us pain.
The open road didn't offer the same

Invitation to us and we'd be insane
To put our trust in the kindness of strangers,
Which would subject us to all kinds of dangers

That never entered the minds of the framers
Of your Constitution, since then we were slaves
Who were born already buried in our graves,

And not even our resurrection saves
Us from evil lurking in the dark places
Of minds that worship the fantasy of races

In the color of skins that nothing erases.
I know you think the colors are projected
But consider those whose lives are inflected

Comedy, Book Three

By the gaze of white people long since infected
By the disease of an irrational hate
That sometimes may seem dormant but just you wait—

When you begin to feel you're safe, it awakes.
So black folks don't feel safe in their common life
For fear they won't see coming the murderous eye

Whose evil gaze caused Emmett Till to die.
Since our time together we've both grown old,
But for you horizons expanded on the road

While for me each joy seemed like a death foretold.
I married when I was young and had a child,
A daughter whose love forced me to tame my wild

Passions, and she and my wife together filed
Away the jagged edges of my soul,
And I watched her grow up and achieve her goal

To become a doctor at the U of Chicago
And travel all over the world to help save lives
That might be lost, and then another thrived

In the military where he enjoyed the pride
I never knew, but in a war he died
From a stray bullet and no one knew which side

It came from, but the military lied
Until his crew gave us the truth undyed.
My third child was a boy everyone loved

But in South Chicago he got the fatal shove
Into death because he was in the wrong place
And the cop didn't see the soul, just the race,

Or how me and my wife would be laid to waste.
In my fifties I died, and my wife and daughter cried
But before I passed my grandson had arrived

Canto 13

And heaven was knowing he'd lead a different life,
For though things had not changed as much as I'd like,
I felt there was a light on the horizon

And hope was an act of will to keep your eyes on
That dream like we were taught by Doctor King.
But though the fate of being black can bring

On suffering, it can cause souls to take wing
And find joy in the incommensurate thing,
Like Charlie Parker's sax that echoes life's

Syncopations or just a plate of my wife's
Fried chicken or watching my grandson break dance,
Because there is no sorrow without the chance

Of a glorious vision of the human expanse,
The negation of a negation I guess you'd say,
Just knowing things don't have to be this way,

And life's scars point you toward the Judgment Day,
But that's not about evening the score,
Just the illumination that would restore

The primal vision from that other shore,
The place of innocence that experience
Covered with the detritus of common sense

That can be redeemed through common intelligence,
Which means thinking through the song of multitude.
Brother, no race exists in solitude

No matter how hard it may try to exclude
The other, because just as I live in your brain,
Some part of everyone will always remain

In everyone else, which means the human domain
Expands forever, and forever the reign
Of truth will find its voice and sing the blues.

Comedy, Book Three

So I've come to you now to speak these truths
And to redeem what was lost in our youths,
Though everything lost leaves a trace in the mind."

"That trace," I said, "can never be left behind."

CANTO 14

The nameless one from my past walked on and I
Thought him not one but many with whom my life
Intersected, who were now a part of me

And whom I now in retrospect could see
More clearly illuminated by history.
Then I grabbed the ladder and climbed back up to the airship

To continue through the light fantastic my trip,
And as Cosmo hauled the ladder in, he said,
"Everyone you've known lives in your head

With a few like me who live in books you've read.
Though we're not real, the brain from which we came
Wears us like a mask in order to proclaim

The absurdity of a world in which the reign
Of injustice drives the multitude insane,
Until a fragment follows the inane,

With each member imprinted just the same
And no trace of singularity remains.
Now grab ahold as we're about to blast

Through time and space to a place where you were cast
By chance that led to your *vita nuova*."
On the instant out of nowhere arose a

Mental wind with such force that could blow a
Mind out of stagnation, toward a destination
That was the site of my regeneration

After the years of my long probation.
When Santa Cruz came in sight, mixed memories
Flooded my mind—some joys and some miseries,

But life shines bright through its negativities,
Like columns of light streaking across night skies,
And every progression is an act that defies

Comedy, Book Three

The crushing waves that threaten to capsize
The fragile skiff that barely stays afloat
Unless through acts of will that seize on hope

The mind fortifies itself in revolt.
The airship descended into the ascending field
Next to Hagar Drive, which once unconcealed

Possibilities of freedom that almost healed
The open wounds that my spirit still bore.
I waved farewell to the Chums off to explore

Mental geographies on other shores
Of transindividual thought, intersections
Of minds that energized my affections

And better than any guide gave me directions.
I followed Hagar up to where a trail
Wedged in by paved progress thoughtlessly assailed

Memories of walks in the quiet woods that prevailed
Once, reminding me nothing stays the same,
But I didn't feel the necessity of blame,

For against the destruction of the past to declaim
Is nostalgia that cuts time's throat and kills
The future that from present immanence distills

The essence of a constellation of wills.
On the path taken I came to the old library
Where for hours on hours I used to bury

Myself, but in front sat one whom I would barely
Believe was real, if already so many dead
Had not spoken to me—then this one said,

"I never knew what an outrageous red
You are, until now that I'm in your head.
I told you you're going in the wrong direction

Canto 14

When your reading of Joyce felt like a dissection—
I mean what need was there to put his bowels
On display, though now I'll make my avowals—

How could I judge any of your words as vile
When I knew how alike are art and shit,
Which Joyce in *Finnegans Wake* had to admit,

And Freud had already suggested it?
(Did I feel slighted by francophonies,
Or fear your seduction by macaronies,

Enamored as you were by all the cronies
Of Hayden White, whom he convinced to write
Letters supporting your claim to a Fulbright—

What do you take me for? some halfwit wight!)
No matter what I said you had to pursue
The thought at the time that seemed like truth to you,

Yet that truth never stands still but passes through,
And that's the best I can say about you.
Though you were a dreamer who lived in a cave,

You came into the light on a quest to save,
Not the self in the cave but the self as essence
Of the many-authored reality, the presence

Of the multitude's visionary florescence
By becoming conscious in the waking dream,
The dead dream's wake when Finnegans wake redeemed—

Not by idols who declare their lies supreme,
The Santissimos who trump the cave as a grave
With morality and money to enslave

Poetic minds until the end of days,
For everyone's a poet when they try
To build heaven in hell and look awry

Comedy, Book Three

On all the false gods that cover the eye.
Redemption is continuous creation
That marries labor to imagination

And every poem a secular revelation—
But poetry is not just words but act,
Like schizophrenia, which is not a lack

In the body of reason but an attack
Against the fortress of sanctimony,
Or holy money your mother saw in phony

Religious schemes that sought to impose atony
Of the soul, countered by her dissonant symphony,
Negation's negation through imagination,

Though she barely understood her own creation—
Prophets envision what they don't understand,
But in other minds time itself lends a hand,

And through minute steps slowly thought expands.
Her visions are the source from which you spring—
Even this dream circles back like a ring

Binding your voice to hers in the song you sing,
But remember that song can't express everything
Since infinite truth exceeds your finite grasp.

To touch it and know it's there is the sacred task
Of art, seeing the whole in a minute part,
Blake's grain of sand, but no vision can chart

The whole—to map it is like trying to cart
Time through space and can only obfuscate
The rolling river of truth that can't abate—

Perpetual motion is its permanent state.
That's why I wonder about your communism,
And despite my sympathies—don't all its schisms

Canto 14

Betray what I called fraternal Marxism?
Without a democratic apparatus,
All it erects is a giant phallus,

And the multitude becomes only ballast
To stabilize the power of the one—
Be it man or party who holds the gun

That puts fear into the soul of everyone.
Your multitude was my unification
Of the human race, which was even embraced

By Pope John to whom you once prayed for grace
To save you from a thought you could not escape,
Though you were just a child who feared the worse,

That you might become a communist and be cursed."
"Nobby," I finally said, "something in me,
Though young and ignorant, could not fail to see

A world populated by the unfree
Everywhere I looked, from my own family
To every soul who had to work for their bread

Or like my mom to serve a man instead,
Or like black people of whom my grandma said—
They do most of the work for which they're bled

Of human dignity by whites who dread
The day black folks speak as one to say, 'No!'
And the powerful will need a new domino

Theory when across the universe the echo
Of that no becomes the multitude's canto.
But that glorious day has already begun

And however long it takes it will be won."

CANTO 15

Then Nobby said, "Why use the word 'communist'
After events that have made the word ominous
In minds that counter dogma with dogma

And imagine wealth a gift from above the
Secular world, divinely sanctioned by God
Or nature or luck, names for the common lot

Of lives that may rise up or rot and rot?
Money is holy to those who don't have it,
And those who do are addicted to profit,

Like children who can't stop playing with their shit—
Because that's what money is, a fetish,
Made out of wastes we reshape and embellish

Until value itself becomes hellish,
Human wastes smeared over the human face
When people see shit as a form of grace

And fight for their fair share of the thing most base.
But what is communism when driven by hate
And revenge rather than the desire to create

A social body that would incorporate
Everyone's power through mutual forgiveness—
Not to control or standardize, but to bless

And solicit what each can contribute to progress—
Permanent revolution, permanent creation,
That pressupposes the commensuration

Of the incommensurate in liberation
Of unique powers each individual stores
In body and intellect that can open doors

To a future in which only poetic wars
Take place and no one dies in the mental fight
To determine between contraries what must be right

Canto 15

For the multitude—in the name of love, not spite.
Mutual forgiveness must mean compromise,
Which is not to settle for less oppressive lies

But a step in the truth process to communize
The multitude, to liberate desires
By forming a constellation that aspires

Not to dominate others but to inspire,
To breathe in the desire of the other
As the force that enables you to discover

Truth that lies beyond objects that cover
Desire's true aim, the thing that has no name—
Call it a river that never stays the same

As it flows into an unbounded infinite main."
"Nobby," I said, "the world has changed since the days
Of Marx, and though his critiques are like x-rays—

Exposing hidden rules capital obeys,
Structures that warp human desire in ways
That turn humans into unconscious slaves—

They couldn't predict that the capitalist phase
Of human history would last so long or raise
Life's quality, which it would then debase—

Not just through exploitation that seeks to raze
The fortress of a common will to be free—
But through fictions of individuality

That stamp each person like a commodity
With illusions that take away their autonomy
When their difference is like everyone else's

And they resent any difference that possesses
A difference from their own, which alienates
The multitude from itself when each one hates

Comedy, Book Three

What's not in their own image and that creates
Divisions that supersede calls to unity
And negate the being of greater community,

Which also negates individuality.
The most singular self is a multiplicity
Of selves but never an imitation,

Which only counterfeits congregation
And subverts the power of cooperation
By subordinating multitude to the one—

One man, one nation, one imagination,
One dream, one theme, one interpretation,
One God, one law, one civilization,

One sex, one race, one class—against the not-one,
Neither imitation nor approximation,
But a living force that counts each difference the same.

The true unity has no singular name
Because it has no identity when it acts
Like heavenly bodies that interact

In constellations that confront the lack
Of light with the glory of a starry night,
For the multitude casts off the One as a blight

That plagues the harvest of each particular light,
The specific powers that each soul brings to bear
On transindividual thoughts and acts they share

In a movement driven by the power of care.
The cold logic of Marx's voice conveyed
To some a cruelty that led to acts that betrayed

The power of care that fueled his own crusade,
And Marx became an angry God whose wrath
Could justify a political blood bath

Canto 15

Led by revolutionaries on a path
Narrow and bordered by walls of dogma
That step by step created bad karma

Through terror that became the daily drama
Of self-justifying dictatorship
Of the One that the multitude learned to worship

Out of fear that kept it firmly in the grip
Of a state that far from withering away
In the name of the working class postponed the day

Of workers' empowerment and then that state
Declared itself communism by decree
And anyone who dared to disagree

Was arrested as a spy of the bourgeosie.
Finally, bad karma like a tidal wave
Swept away the party and over its grave

Erected a new capitalism that behaves
Like a dictatorship of the kleptocrats,
Or the party's bureaucrats put on new hats

And become capitalism's latest autocrats,
But in both cases the multitude loses
And pays a price for all the abuses

Of a revolution that vengeance seduces
Into the practice of violent negation
Instead of forgiveness and persuasion.

Aufhebung never meant annihilation,
And killing the bourgeoisie can never achieve
The communism the multitude must weave

Out of its own understanding that conceives
Like new life a different world within reach
When the multitude simply learns how to teach

Itself through introspection—not to impeach
Itself or others who may disagree
Nor to force a false and fatal unity

That always builds walls around community
But to treat each singular soul like a seed
That from its outer cover must be freed

Through nurturing practices that feed and knead
It until its immanent being bursts forth
Through the liberation of powers that force

True individuation to take its course.
But the power of each requires the power of all,
No one is free who lives behind a wall

Like an infant child who's delivered en caul—
Knocking the wall down is self-transcendence,
The first step toward love's interdependence,

The power of multitude in ascendance.
Communism is not just state ownership
And never the triumph of class dictatorship

In a so-called worker's state firmly in the grip
Of a fragment that covers the infinity
Of the multitude, the only divinity

That gathers all human singularities
Together in the rule of the not-one.
Communism's permanent revolution

Is the struggle for democracy that's won
When no vital being feels forgotten
And the voice of everyone is finally heard

In the word made flesh and the flesh that speaks the word."

CANTO 16

"How do you get to communism without
A state, and do you mean to disavow
Public ownership as the antidote

To private property that leads to a bloat
In the wealth of a few that becomes a crushing weight
On the multitude and in that way negates

Their communion through endless war and debate
Over who gets what from what falls from the plate
Of those who own the political system

And claim for themselves a patent on wisdom?
Communism is love's body, which I implied
When I searched for a way to reverse the tide

Of the nuclear death wish that seemed to ride
The wild horses of capitalist desire,
Itself determined to set the world on fire

As the moneymen burn with the need to acquire
Ownership not just of worktime and place
But any desire that interferes with their race

Against spontaneity they want to encase
Like a commodity that must lay waste
To desire's truth, the essence beyond exchange,

Beyond objects so carefully arranged
To obfuscate the light of will-less grace,
Like rhyming lines that force the mind to embrace

Unforeseen thoughts the unconscious conveys.
The state becomes the antithesis of grace
When it makes a fetish out of power—

Because true power is like a spring shower
That spreads like a curtain across nature's bower,
Animating with life the seeds that flower

Comedy, Book Three

In diffuse being that celebrates the hour
Resurrecting the living and the dead—
But the state too often with a blanket of dread

Covers the multitude until it's bled
Of autonomy that lies immanent to the all—
The collective body the state would keep in thrall

And make cooperation against the law
If it subverts a reality bourgeois—
Then the state becomes a manacle that binds

Individualities into a blind
Submission to one law, one truth, one God—
And justice itself is nothing more than a rod

To punish the soul that thinks it's more than a clod.
What hope is there for communist desire
If it requires the state to stoke the fire

That it can also make into a pyre
That burns love's body until only ashes
Blowing in the wind remain of what the masses

Dream when they search for what surpasses
The drudgery of wage slavery and the war
Of all against all that negates the rapport

That measures a power that would forevermore
Rule iself if the multitude were free
To express its being in true democracy

Instead of believing the lies of autocracy.
In your brain I see how bad things have become
Of late, as it seems excessive wealth has won

And forced the multitude to turn a gun
On itself, which keeps everyone on the run."
So spoke the spirit of Norman O. Brown,

Canto 16

Though I could tell that voice was also bound
To my own, because the feeling of despair
Echoed my own sense of the lack of care

That showed itself in acts that would forswear
Too often the communion that could empower
The multitude to act and seize the hour

And through cooperation not to cower
Before the voice that says nothing can change
And too much hope causes you to estrange

Yourself from realities perfectly arranged.
But I felt the power of hope and said:
"Your voice and mine interweave like two threads,

Which together form a mental web in my head
With other voices both living and dead,
And this constellation like a rainbow

Is the promise that refuses to let go
Of hope and finds signs of it everywhere.
Music and cinema mutually share

Unconscious truths—even in a nightmare,
Like the Kafka-inspired story of a man who fused
Himself with a fly but then became confused

Between the insect and the man who used
To be torn between jealous passion and science,
But the conflict was resolved with defiance

When the insect chose its own self-reliance
And dismissed the life of a man as just the dream
Of an insect who now awoke to a regime

Of cruelty and didn't hear the others scream.
We are insects when we submit to a scheme
That feeds on the flesh of other human beings

Comedy, Book Three

And in the process kill our own feelings—
But to know the worst of what humans can be
Gives us the power to challenge that destiny.

Cinematic horrors' popularity
Is not a sign of human depravity
But the culture's unconscious manifesto

Of a common thought that could be made to grow
Into a form of critical self-awareness
That belongs to a multitude that would harness

All its individualities to progress
Without end, for every specific goal
Is a steppingstone toward an uncountable whole,

Which the state facilitates but cannot control.
The Civil Rights Movement said—Keep your eyes
On the prize, which was not one law but to revise

A reality founded on a set of lies,
And the only test of success is democracy's
Expansion of individualities

And the realization of equalities—
Not identity but greater autonomy,
Not judged by the growth-rate of an economy,

But the power of each to be what they want to be.
The long revolution is experiment,
And if social ownership works, then it's meant

To be, but if it becomes an impediment,
Then cast aside dogma and theory and try
Something else, for what makes things go awry

Is self-righteousness that covers the eye
And clogs the ear so that no one sees or hears
What people may be saying with their tears

Canto 16

Or when they march and shout and cheer their peers.
But none of this can ever come to be
Without the freedom of real democracy

And the right to speak truth with complete liberty,
Understanding that truth is not closure
But within a process of thought the cynosure

That fuels lifelong commitment to exposure
Of the power of human cooperation
That could lead to a secular reformation.

To those on the left who call reform evasion
If not betrayal of communism's foundation,
Look to the Marxist Negri who said the whole

Consists of parts, not countable like a toll,
But in the relation between parts lies the soul
Of revolution or reform unless

Either declares the finitude of the process,
Which the state itself subsumes and then outlaws
Any voice that speaks out for a new cause

In the effort to put the multitude on pause."
Then Nobby spoke: "I once called you a mensch,
Because you didn't allow me to entrench

On your thought driven by passion that seemed intense,
But now I see that mensch is a thing common
That lies dormant in the heart of everyone

And awakening the mensch is resurrection,
But this event must continually repeat
Itself because the mensch drifts into sleep

In the fantasy of its own private keep."

CANTO 17

I then replied, "The mind sometimes needs rest,
As in Blake's Beulah, a place where souls are blessed
With regenerating sleep before the test

Of mental war against forces that repress
Creative imagination because it foresees
Unlimited human possibilities

With the power of elective affinities
To produce energy more than the sum of parts,
And one connection to others comes through the arts,

Including popular culture that imparts
Through minute steps unsolicited thought,
Setting the mind on fire until it's brought

To the boiling point where something new is wrought,
And even the most distracted spectator
May engage in unconscious mental labor

That becomes the chrysalis of a new creator.
But the error we make in closing our mental eyes
Is thinking permanent sleep a paradise,

A world without conflict where no one dies,
But the real heaven is the eternal dance
Of the contaries, not a vapid romance—

Creation and sleep alternate and enhance
Each other, unless we make them negations,
Then mental war becomes extermination,

And sleep withdrawal and numbing isolation.
Nobby, for me at times this place was Beulah
When these trees chanted joyous hallelujahs,

And at other times it became a school of
Intellectual war, not with the aim to kill
But to engage in militant love with a will

Canto 17

To process disagreement and distill
From it cooperation that empowers
Both parties, yours and mine becoming ours,

As contraries transform minutes and hours
Into infinite sequences that incorporate
Continuous revisions and translate

Emerging desires that never come too late."
"I see now that we were true contraries,"
Nobby said, "and though Jameson was wary

Of your challenges that to him seemed to carry
Some disrespect, what drove you was opposite
To that, admiration quite immoderate

Of a thought process seemingly confederate
With your own political desire, and the voice
Of your opposition expressed the choice

Of true friendship in which your soul rejoiced.
'Without contraries is no progression,'
Wrote Blake, and his poetry taught you a lesson—

While contraries may drift into negation,
Forgiveness of self and others must sublate
What fell apart and in time recreate

The intellectual struggle that won't abate
Until through continuous resurrections
Of a truth that lives on through supersessions,

The multitude produces progressions
That express the energy of creative love.
But now I must give you a little shove,

For I hear voices calling not from above,
But in your brain they're telling you to come
And to be careful not to naively succumb

Comedy, Book Three

To the backward gaze of nostalgic seduction."
As we separated and I walked away,
His last words awoke the memory of a day

When with excitement I had myself conveyed
By bus to the Rio Theater and saw
A movie that strangely filled my eyes with awe,

Though I could see it was horribly flawed,
But there was beauty I could not ignore,
Not just images but the story of a war

That in Wyoming between the rich and the poor
Took place—then suddenly in front of the Rio
On Soquel I stood, faced with Michael Cimino

Who had something he wanted me to know
About what in my memory still persisted,
The idea that too often movies consisted

Of nostagia for a past that never existed—
Bertolucci said that, but it didn't mean
There was no truth in what they put on the screen.

"Nostalgia," Michael said, "lures us to a scene
That makes the vision of history a dream,
But from this nightmare we can finally awake

To recognition of desires at stake
Surviving in traces of forgotten lives,
Shadows of the past that in some ways are lies,

But when they appear on screens in forms that surprise
Consciousness with images that resonate
With present corruptions that must perpetuate

Events that came before that necessitate
The world now, then the screen becomes an eye
That we see through, not with, looking awry

Canto 17

Until truth is revealed on the other side.
The real Jim Averell and Ella Watson
Were hanged and left to swing in the hot sun,

And the reason was private property in Johnson
County, Wyoming, where they got in the way
Of men for whom human life can't outweigh

Property and wealth in the balance to which they pray,
Because money's their God and they hold sway
Over the law and still do to this day

Since there's justice only for those who pay.
My Averill fought with the multitude against
The power of wealth that wanted the West unfenced

Because it belonged to them one hundred percent—
But he was also one of them, the elite,
And he went out west like Roosevelt to complete

His education—and it was quite a feat
To make a Western movie that contains
The sensibility of Henry James

With a hero who doesn't ride off like the Shanes
But retreats into a cage his wealth constructs
On a yacht at sea that effectively deconstructs

The masculinist fantasy that obstructs
The multitude's self-valorization,
Though there's a glimpse of that in Nate Champion,

Who transforms his log cabin into a salon
And treats Ella the whore like a paragon
Of feminine virtue, but unlike Shane

Or the real Nate, this one's first act is profane,
When he murders people like himself for gain,
But his redemption is also his death

Comedy, Book Three

When he regains the honor he had left.
You saw the butchered version of my movie
Here at the Rio, but glimpses of beauty

Touched you and caused you to feel some duty
To witness what the power of money destroyed
And it wouldn't have taken a Sigmund Freud

To see it left me hanging in the void.
They did the same thing to Sam Peckinpah's
Billy the Kid movie that shows how the law's

A funny thing whenever it's the cause
Of injustice, and there's Leone's tale of the West
With a ghostly hero who doesn't invest

In property, but this communist quest
Went against the grain of capitalist bagmen
Who operate like financial gunmen

And shoot down without aesthetic judgment
Any work of art they don't know how to spin—
Add to the number Sergio's Proustian

Gangster film their ignorance saw as fustian
Because it didn't resemble *Godfather*
In the eyes of those who never see farther

Than what it takes to put a quick dollar
In their pocket, which is why Heaven's Gate
Got cut out of the movie *Heaven's Gate*,

But in spite of it all, it's never too late.
One night at the old Sash Mill in Santa Cruz
You felt Leone's masterpiece like the blues,

And the uncut version had to disabuse
Producers and critics who abuse
Their power because they want to screw the muse.

Canto 17

And far from here in Paris you heard the news—
My movie, uncut, at the Cinémathèque
Française, Trocadero, was not a wreck,

But a vision meant to keep false heavens in check."

CANTO 18

"Don't forget Scorsese's *Gangs of New York*,"
I said, "which a few critics wanted to abort,
But he learned something from you and the export

Of the movie quickly saved it from falling short.
Meanwhile all the historians went crazy
And thought the film's handling of facts lazy,

But their blindness to expressive form amazed me—
Sometimes distortions capture history's truth,
But it may take a cinematic sleuth

To unravel the visual web that can induce
The emotional experience of the past—
Not nostalgia but events with shadows cast

On things from dark to dawn that will surpass
All the false heavens that are secretly negations,
Defined by what they exclude—like all nations

Or religions that fail to see hell's their creation.
Blake's heaven is eternal mental war,
Never physical, since it requires a rapport

With eternal forgiveness that must restore
Continually the balance to worlds of thought
That spin like wheels that can never be brought

To a standstill, though sometimes covered by the rot
Of zombie ideas that make thought seem to stop
And allow death to feed on the living form,

The collective body into which we're all born."
"But continuous resurrections fill the gap,"
Cimino said, "and save us from the trap

Of eternal death by teaching us to tap
Into the unquenchable life force that resides
In the will to go on despite obstacles that hide

Canto 18

The end that subsumes all those who have lived and died,
And that end is a truth process without end.
To some our screen violence may seem to commend

Physical war, but the light we take and bend
Onto the eyes of multitude screens mental
Reflections arising from corporeal

Histories of the power that would destroy all
Justice and the dream of freedom in the name
Of a privileged few who claim they own the game

Because private property is all that remains
Of value in the world they would proclaim.
But heaven's gate is human cooperation

Breaking the shackles of exploitation
And forcing the existence of values that transcend
Property when each to each becomes a friend

And the well-being of all becomes the end
Of every political desire, but not
Without failures and betrayals that will block

The path forward, so don't go into shock
If the road to heaven is paved with the stones of hell.
But now it's time for you to say farewell

To this town that once had the power to propel
You to a new life, but still there was more
To learn that took you to another shore

Where with some pain you opened another door."
Then he was gone like in the fog of a dream's
Slow fade-out and a darkness intervened

With only a pinpoint of light barely seen,
But unreal as it was I tried to walk
In that direction but something in me balked,

Comedy, Book Three

Wondering, is this an event that I can chalk
Up to experience and then come back?
But then it came to me, from every lack

In my life a new power to interact
With something greater had come, though like a tunnel
Cold and unlit with power to annul

Vitality and reduce my soul to a dull
Shade of itself it felt to me at first,
Because transition starts off like a curse

When you don't know if it makes things better or worse,
From whence the conservative impulse derives.
But the luminous point gradually gave rise

To an expansive light that guided my eyes,
Until I entered a space I recognized,
For I found myself again on a street in Paris,

A turn of the screw that once enhanced awareness,
On my part, of intellectual passions
That inspired me as well as limitations

That required adjustment and accommodation.
On Rue Lepic above Place Blanche I stood
And everything appeared just as it should

According to my memory, and something good,
My unconscious said, was about to occur.
I went up the street and followed the curve

Until *numéro cinquante* I could observe,
My old address from the years of my poverty,
Though here lack of funds had not bothered me,

Once in this place where French generosity
In the shape of Monsieur Riotte gave us a home.
But from this flood of memories my eye roamed,

Canto 18

And I saw a poorly dressed man all alone
In front of *cinquante-quatre* where Theo
Van Gogh once lived, and then I had to know

This red-haired man I'd seen in his *tableaux*—
It was Vincent and I became absorbed
As he looked up by the sight of his flaming orbs

That engulfed me in his visionary worlds
Where everything emitted its own light
Even under the cover of the night.

Then I said, "For me your stellar art shined bright
In its singularity and your loneliness,
For I could not separate them and confess

I saw my inner being and no less
The soul of my mother in your madness,
Which some called insane but I call inspired,

But inspiration can leave you alone and tired
And haunted by visions no one else can see
Until the weight of human conformity

Crushes the spirit that longs to be free
And share with the world the voice of its destiny."
Then Vincent: "Don't think my life all misery,

Nor my death make into an unsolved mystery,
For the act of creation was my paradise
And now I rest eternally in the eyes

Of everyone who witnesses all the lives
I lived in projected visions that survive
Long after I'm dead, and even when they're gone

To the transindividual mind they'll belong
Because eternity's not endless time
But the immeasurable thought sublime

Comedy, Book Three

That causes every material thing to shine.
One day you'll try to write down all you've seen
In this collective dream, which to you may seem

All your own, but in your thought's endless stream
There is no private property to own
Even if spirit's being is a bone—

As Hegel wrote—a common property grown
In the hot house of perishable human flesh,
Which I touched with my brushstroke's amorous caress,

And if you choose to write you must do no less,
Without concern for public acclamation,
Not now or in some future celebration,

Because all that matters is the revelation,
And even if no one hears your voice
Or from indifference time itself destroys

All the words in which your soul rejoiced,
Remember Blake's prophecy, nothing is lost
And words or images are only dross

Compared with infinite truths that lend their gloss
To what we say and see and then proclaim.
Do Blake or I concern ourselves with fame?

If no one remembered us, it's just the same,
The truth we fought to express would still remain,
Or someone would resurrect that truth again.

I know you've always thought the world had sinned
Against me and made my days living hell,
But thinking that you have wrung my death knell,

So I'm here to confront you and dispel
That sad fantasy about me or your mother—
Yes, our common madness makes us brother

And sister souls mirroring each other."

CANTO 19

"You once wrote 'There is peace even in the storm,'"
    I said to Vincent, "and while I reject the form
    Of your Christian devotion (though I was born

    In a faith, but it left my expectations stillborn
    When it seemed ready to serve the culture of cash,
        Promoting charity while defending class,

Which made the first seem nothing more than a crass
    Cover for those who are bankrupt in spirit—
    So I placed my faith in those who should inherit

Heaven and earth for they have earned this merit
    Through suffering and kindness, which is the soul
        Of multitude but not always the whole,

    For in every ensemble you'll find a hole
    That can undermine foundations like a mole
        If faith loses sight of the expanding frame

    And the possibilities that always remain),
Your words touched me when I read them on a bus
        To California where I placed my trust

    In passion that transcends the chaos of lust,
But like the winds that swept Paolo and Francesca,
    Love's storm broke and I no longer possessed the

    Power to imagine a life beyond the caress of
    The lover whose loss cast me into a void
    Where I fell and fell and thought I was destroyed,

    But then a peace came over me and buoyed
Me up as your words came back to me and I knew
        That love is never lost and feeling blue

    Is prelude to the heaven of the true,
Which is not above or below but here and now.
    Your vision lifted me up and showed me how

To see beyond covers that disallow
The eternity that shines in a sunflower."
"Even if I had lived only an hour,"

He said, "in a seizure of creative power,
It would have been enough to justify
An existence that suffering can't nullify

But rather propels the visionary eye
To see the part of life that cannot die."
Instantly he was gone, leaving me in wonder,

But then in the streets I decided to wander
From Montmartre across Paris to the Rive Gauche
Along a route where I used to feel most close

To the beating heart of the city that arose
From scents of cafés, restos, chocolateries,
And divine pâtisseries and boulangeries

That reached out like a hand to gently squeeze
The heart that passed down the Rue Blanche to the Rue
De la Chausée d'Antin where you can view

Galeries Lafayette Hausmann before one or two
Streets to Place de l'Opéra and its avenue,
Until Rue de Rivoli exposes you

To the torrent of Parisian multitudes.
Through the Louvre's Cour Carrée to the Pont des Arts,
I walked and crossed, gazing leftward at ramparts

Of a holy culture that makes into upstarts
Everything on my side of the ocean,
Because beauty calls you to devotion,

But still it didn't interrupt my motion
As I turned from the Seine toward the Rue Saint-Jacques
And forgot I was in a dream until the shock

Canto 19

Of seeing someone who turned back the clock.
I looked across at the spot where Michel Foucault
Once stood by me waiting for the signal to go

Next to the Collège de France on the Rue des Écoles,
And there he stood again as if in wait
For me, but somehow I feared a debate

Would ensue, for his thought was like a narrow strait
I once had passed through to the ocean beyond
And our visions would no longer correspond,

For truth to me had the force of a bomb,
Which is why truth-sayers to the world seem mad,
Or like some misbegotten Galahad

By their own fantasies easily had,
But the truth of truth is a chain reaction
And every truthful word contains a fraction

Infinitesimal of the whole in action
Without borders to its infinite expansion.
But what in life could not be said straight on

Found in death the breath of inspiration,
And crossing to him I said, "The prison-house
That your discourse both denounced and espoused—

Making truth serve power that disallows
The transformative event out of nowhere
Like when in darkest night at sea a flare

Bursts in the air and forces the being there
Of something unforeseen, but made aware,
A captain changes course under the dictate

Of the seaman's ethical rule that must conflate
The salvation of one with the redemption of all
In the struggle against the sea's power to appall

Comedy, Book Three

The human will with indifference to its law
And institutions that govern what they call
The truth and the illusion of the normal,

That straight path over the abyss scornful
Of nature that exceeds the legislation
That can never master the whole of creation—

The prison of unconscious regulations
Encases the multitude in a world that's fixed,
But it's like a prestidigitator's tricks

Meant to convince us that we're all just bricks
In the wall until we start to call it home
And fear events that speak of the unknown,

Revealing desires that force our minds to roam—"
Then Foucault raised his hand and stopped me with a gaze
That dissected the soul of my thought like an x-ray,

And then to me: "You were once not so brave
When you stood next to me but did not say
What was on your mind, but perhaps you thought

You were invisible to me and ought
Not to violate the decorum of power,
But in your silence and my indifference our

Separate wills didn't submit and lose the hour
Of untried possibility from lack
Of power but enforced the power we lacked

And unconsciously bound ourselves to the rack,
And if our will finds a voice that responds
To social directives with a vagabond

Movement of desire that tries to loosen the bond
That tells us nothing we can do matters,
That resistance to power only shatters

Canto 19

The mirror in which we see ourselves as masters
  Who celebrate a selfhood that negates
  The multitude's power, which it relegates

To nonexistence under the rule of states—
  Then we cast ourselves into a social hell,
  For others hear our voice as the death knell

Of the fantasy of self with which they swell
  And call it freedom—but it's a prison cell.
  Yes, my vision is harsh, but pessimism

  Of the intellect induces optimism
Of the will—and that was Gramsci's communism,
And though some say for Marx I had a distaste,

  It was those who had laid Marxism to waste
    By building brutal authoritarian states
    In his name that set me on a different path,

And you and I both share this critical wrath.
  Like my cohorts, to Mao I gave credence
  Once upon a time, mostly from ignorance,

Which teaches the lesson that so-called brilliance
  Against error offers no insurance.
  In that Maoist crew was Alain Badiou

From whom you derive a philosophy of the true,
Despite his allegiance to Mao's name that to you
  Reads like some kind of mental myopia

  That projects paradise onto dystopia.
  But forgive us our errors as we forgive
  Yours, for the essence of thought may outlive

  Impurities once filtered through the sieve
Of time that might be called eternity's dredge.
  Everything we write has a double edge

  That cuts against its own temporal cortège."

CANTO 20

Foucault continued, "There's something in your mind—
A thought from a past that you can't leave behind,
And I coexist with that thought and understand

Why for you it constitutes a demand
For an answer over which you have command—
As old Lacan might say—that stops desire,

Which you experience like a high wire
On which you balance yourself but cannot see
Where it starts or ends, which means you can't breathe free

Without the fear of falling into the debris
Of broken lives and the void where they all end.
But I'll say this, you can't escape or transcend

A truth that life forced you to apprehend,
And desire is the engine of the truth process
That causes categories to evanesce

Despite institutions that acquiesce
In final judgments that put the case to rest.
For you permanent tension between two words

Creates a force that constantly disturbs
The memory of one who opened the door
To the heaven of thought that rests upon the floor

Of hell's finitude perpetually at war
With the power of imagination to soar
Above the flat earth of rote mentality

That dams the flow of thought with morality,
A program that bypasses the ethical choice
Without which freedom lacks the power to voice

A desire that exceeds the mirrored self and deploys
The being of multitude as the greater mind
That through cooperation becomes divine

Canto 20

And into the ethical void its light must shine
With the immanence of its secular revelation.
The two words that sparked your education

And a history of constant vacillation
Are 'mad' and 'insane,' the latter implying the pain
Of clinical mental illness that left a stain

On a soul whose intellectual domain
Extended toward the gates of paradise,
While the first word speaks to how you were surprised

By the truth of a vision that lifted the veil of lies
That covered the true worth of every common
Soul no matter how low and downtrodden

Or secure in the privileges of a brahman.
Her vision penetrated delusions of class
And race and to everyone she gave a pass

And gathered like so many leaves of grass
Every singular soul who crossed her path,
For she had felt the world's cruelty and wrath

At anyone whose difference makes them laugh,
Not from joy that derives from love but mean
Pleasure from others' suffering that comes from spleen

And expresses self-hate by themselves unseen.
This was your mother whom people called insane,
But to you such dismissive labels are inane,

Since at least madness has a history both profane
And divine that makes it the most common name
For poetic vision no category

Can veil from revealing its singular glory,
Expressing truth that alters every story
By forcing inclusion of what has been left out

Comedy, Book Three

And shows the multitude a different route
To the future, which is the gift of every prophet.
But in a world whose supreme value is profit,

    Visionaries are dragged onto the docket
    And judged as either evil or insane,
Then locked in a cage with bars that may remain

    Invisible but nonetheless contain
    The intellectual edge of a luminal
Eye that rips the veil from what seems nouminal

    But lies immanent in every phenomenal
    Sensation that ideology covers
Like wild kudzu, and that was your mother's

Gift and curse, when she felt a truth that suffers
From a world that sees vision as monstrosity
    And misconstrues love as animosity

    Onto which it projects its own hypocrisy,
And sometimes prophets lack the words to fight
The power that wants to chase them into the night,

    But what words cannot say the body will write
    On itself and divine madness becomes disease,
And then death finally comes but cannot appease

The fire that burns through covers like dead leaves,
    Because no singular body stands alone
And from flesh to flesh creates its eternal home.

    By the wind of love to you the fire was blown
    And your task is to find the words that spread
    Abroad the burning seeds that can be read

    By generations or by one whose head
Catches fire with what passes through your own.
Your body and brain are more than her epigone,

Canto 20

But through their mediation her being has grown
    Beyond the life of her body and its errors,
  For sometimes suffering broadcasts its terrors

    Toward the innocent who are bearers
      Of a love that fear transforms into cruel
  Judgments of those who look for her approval

    But cannot see what she has seen of brutal
      Existence, and prophets are often most blind
To those whose lives with their own are intertwined,

    Like when Jesus told his mother to mind
      Her own business and on her cast a cold eye.
  Prophets are not predictors but voices that cry

    Out in the wilderness against the lie,
  But that doesn't mean they can see on every side.
  Your mother's truth survives her imperfections,

And yours will survive despite your own defections.
    Divine madness is not mystical but human,
    Not transcendent but what you name common,

  For what we mean by divine is what comes from
      The multitude—there is no other God.
    Every act that seeks to improve the lot

    Of all the others tears down the facade
      Of false categories that keep us separate
    Until powerlessness makes us desperate

    For a world beyond the reign of the disparate.
      In all her children she planted this dream
    And taught forgiveness in the way she seemed

To love your father whom you sometimes deemed
    Unforgivable, but she could see the worth
    In every soul who wandered upon the earth

Comedy, Book Three

And her compassion never knew a dearth.
Her sins were the sins of unbounded love
But her eye was not confined to what's above

But looked down at what power has rebuffed."
Then I to him: "Are you the real Foucault,
For your writing was impersonal and cold,

I mean always analytical, controlled—
What if anything to you was divine?"
He answered, "Everything that exists in time

Has a history with the power to refine
Its truth, and the modern clinical idea
Cannot subsume and erase what would be a

Divine spectacle to those who can see a
Meaning that breaks the circle of opinions
That dominates and circumscribes billions

Who live unconsciously in the dominions
Of common sense and who like to forget history
And bathe themselves in the joys of pure mystery.

Jesus was mad to challenge some consistory
With teachings that ignored their authority,
But like Lacan said, only the non-duped err.

Jesus like your mother was too aware
Of things others ignored that consumed his care,
And caring too much is an attribute of the mad.

Sometimes their loneliness makes them feel sad,
And other times they are joyous and glad.
Call it manic-depression if you want

But their visions will continue to haunt
The future and for you they will align,
For though those souls aren't gods they are divine

And live in the paradise of a common mind."

CANTO 21

"Common mind, common sense, what's the difference?"
I asked, and Foucault: "The latter does violence
To the first when it eradicates process

And congeals thought into a dam against progress—
Which doesn't mean the end at which life aims,
But continuous motion of thought and act that sustains

A truth that exceeds every context and remains
Always incomplete but leaving traces
That condition ethical actions in the spaces

Of everyday life with common graces
Unless they are bent into perverse dogma
And the flow of thought becomes frozen magma,

Making truth itself into a stigma,
A disease like madness that says what everyone knows
But no one speaks for fear it will expose

Untamed desires like the murder of crows
That in Hitchcock's dream were bent on murder.
But now one awaits whose rational fervor

Inspired your writing and moved the cursor
Of your life to unexpected locations
That were the birthplace of your vocation,

Though his critique aroused my irritation
And caused me to see him as my enemy
When I should have recognized my contrary,

But intellectual pride made me wary.
'Opposition is true friendship,' Blake said,
And now that Jacques and I are both quite dead,

I see the marriage of our thought in your head,
Which to some reads like discourses of the mad,
But the intellectual challenge made you glad

Comedy, Book Three

And even Lacan to you was more than a fad—
Yes, reason has its own modes of *jouissance*."
Then the light on Rue des Écoles changed and at once

He walked away though in my head he's ensconced
Like all the others on these visitations.
So I continued my peregrination

Down the Rue Saint-Jacques toward my destination.
I crossed the Place du Panthéon and went
Down Rue d'Ulm to the École where once I spent

Time with the man whose thought was an ascent
Toward truth through a descent into the texture
Of writing as interwoven gestures

Of words like threads forming more than a vesture
That covers a thing like magic that would reveal
The essence of what it also must conceal—

No, the fabric of discourse has no ideal
But spreads out like the galaxy beyond
Measure and each word like a star must respond

To lines of determination like a bond
That is itself bound to an infinite set
Of relations that constantly beget

New relations that generate like a debt
Constantly postponed meanings incomplete
Like payments of interest that won't deplete

The principal that sustains itself in retreat,
For the infinite truth is always out of reach
Except as process that leaves traces that teach

Patience and responsibility for each
Decision and its unforeseen consequences
Should old definitions become senseless,

Canto 21

Creating the need for revision of premises.
With these thoughts I came to the gate of École Normale
Supérieure and soon went down a hall

And then up to the *premier étage* where I saw
The site of my infrequent visitations
With one whose kindness exceeded my expectations

As I struggled to explain my dissertation,
But now as I glanced through the open door,
I saw the man who had died some years before,

But in this mental space I knew that more
In the mode of revelation would come my way.
Then he said, "Come in and sit without delay,

As we examine your mental dossier,
Now that I've unlimited time and no wall
Of language comes between us to forestall

Communication—since as you may recall,
We agreed that I'd speak French and you English,
Though my motive was somewhat surreptitious

As about the French language I was religious
And couldn't stand to hear any misuse—"
"And my speech subjected it to some abuse,"

I interjected, "self-consciousness induced
A stumbling grammar I hardly overcame,
But you never made me feel any shame

Unlike another who could not refrain
From letting me know I didn't belong in her course,
But I submerged myself in your discourse,

In the untranslated books that I perforce
Read in your tongue, not a *terra incognita*
Anymore than those of Julia Kristeva

Comedy, Book Three

Whose snobbery was so unlike Derrida
Though you had as much cause to be like her."
Then he to me: "Though you couldn't abide her,

She like the two of us was an outsider,
And everyone negotiates differences
Differently—but don't interpret those dissonances

Of character as all that her essence is.
She opened the first door to Joyce's project
For you, when she made you see the subject

As process, and then summoned like a ghost the abject
In which you saw your own writing as the trace
Of your mother that her death could not erase,

Like a waste product that contained a grace,
And you channeled it through vagaries of style,
Your own, which seemed to some formless and wild,

But it was language itself you put on trial,
And through multiple experiments you sought
To conquer the abject in language that wrought

Your own subjectivity as something fraught,
Haunted by the maternal voice that's thought
By all but you to be clinical madness

Because they felt its eternal sadness,
But that was only a shadow cast by the light
Of a vision that gave shape to a world more bright

In the faith that there's such a thing as the right.
In my own work you thought you heard again
The madness of truth that some saw as a sin,

Empty words blown about by a fatuous wind,
But when you discovered my friendly enemy,
Badiou, his discourse felt like a remedy

Canto 21

To the problem of how a decision to act ethically
Can contain the force of truth without closure
As it undergoes revision through exposure

To boundless context, which compels moreover
Responsibility without limit.
But Badiou could see something there I didn't—

Readings that forced something inexistent
To exist, like the ghostly ideas that haunt
The discourses that exclude the other and flaunt

Their transcendence of that from which they must launch
Their own conceptual being, their essence,
Which always contains within itself a presence

Alien that was refused coalescence
But remains the inescapable shadow,
The spectrality that contaminates the whole

Until essence itself becomes a hole,
The incompleteness that will not let go
Of the blind power that sleepwalks in a trance

Until the shadow takes the lead in a dance
That turns over the place of non-being
To reveal the place of unforeseen seeing

Where the other tears the veil of power's seeming
And steps through it into the greater expanse
Of a world to-come, the promise of a manse

That houses everyone—call it the advance
Of true democracy, which was my stance
That Badiou called the *passion of Inexistance*,

But don't think it was a dreamy romance.
To open a door is never the end of a fight
And every new light puts a shadow to flight—

There is no final act to the play of the right."

CANTO 22

"Jacques Derrida, as strange as it may seem,"
I said, "you occupy the place in my dream
Of intellectual love because between

The lines of your writing another scene
Played out, behind the fire of your critique
That alienated some from your technique

That made love to a text in ways oblique
Like a socratic midwife who gives birth
To what remains in excess by exposing the dearth

In what's been written with a force to unearth
Another ground from which innovation
Arises, the permanent continuation

That generates newness through reformation
Without end, but anyone touched by your gaze,
However critical, should feel the rays

Of amorous delight that amount to praise.
Yet I use the concept of reform which some
See as a copout because they want a gun

To settle the score before the day has been won,
But one whose Marxism you might not embrace
Saw in reform more than a temporal waste

But a consistency of steps that displace
The foundation to make room for the *to-come*,
A teleology of the common,

And though *telos* may be for you a problem,
Its meaning here is not some future One,
The end that comes before it has begun,

But closer to your democracy to come,
And the common may be your minimal consensus
That sometimes may seem utterly senseless

Canto 22

When it drifts in ways that may prevent us
From finalization because like reason it
Has no reason and appears only the gift

Of that which answers the call of the *es gibt*.
Antonio Negri's the one to whom I refer
And to his love of Spinoza I defer,

Whose concept of democracy would concur
With your own if one understands the *to-come*
As the always-coming that time itself can't plumb

Or predetermine what it may become.
Intellectual love is the love of truth,
And if you became a kind of textual sleuth

Who could unravel the threads and follow the clues
That led to the scene of what each text excludes—
It was not the will to destroy or to abuse,

Not to create enemies or to confuse,
But to find the traces of truths that disappear
With every effort to finalize the frontier

Like when nations close their borders from fear
Of the strangers who come bearing voices from elsewhere—
To some a *déclaration de guerre*,

As if they might contaminate the air
With the breath of languages speaking histories
That haunt the nation like unsolved mysteries,

Forcing memories of unspeakable cruelties,
But the truth written in the flesh of those who come
Takes mystery out of the dark until it becomes

The light of multitude that brings everyone
Into the shelter not to fade away—
But the dark is always just a shot away,

Comedy, Book Three

And redemption always just a kiss away,
According to the secular gospel of Mick,
And sometimes common language does the trick

To bring us back to paradise in the nick
Of time, back to Joyce's 'communionism,'
Or as I would like to write it, coming-ism,

Echoes of what should have been communism."
Then Derrida: "The place I must occupy
In your brain cannot entirely disqualify

Your will to rewrite, though perhaps my watchful eye
In life might have paid you greater tribute
And friendship with a reading not to refute

But to mark traces of an alternate route,
Possibilities your thoughtful but rough edged
Readings barely touched but at least they pledged

Themselves to a future reading that might dredge
From Joyce's styles like layers you excavate,
A void so expansive it may innovate

An archaeology of the infinite wake,
Of a past always becoming without break
A possible future of what it will have been,

The place where past becoming begins again.
When you appeared in my office that day
In a homespun jacket your wife had made,

I thought you a vagabond come to invade
My space, which amused more than it made me afraid,
But you reminded me of who you were

And then made a request I'd have preferred
You had not—to attend a seminar you'd heard
About for Yale students but I'd incurred

Canto 22

Contractual obligations, to which I referred,
That forced me to limit the attendance,
Which now causes me to feel some repentance,

Because I might have lacked certain cognizance
Of how, despite their dreams of equality,
Americans enjoy exclusivity,

Though how could I have done things much differently?"
To which I replied, "Forgive me if I was brash,
But I owed it to myself at least to ask.

A more positive answer would have unmasked
My boldness because in truth I was afraid
That too much exposure would have betrayed

The void that lay behind my masquerade.
My being there was itself an act of will,
Overcoming the sense that had been drilled

Into me of worthlessness I struggled to kill
My whole life, but that also gave me the shove
To push beyond what I was capable of

And pursue something unsayable out of love—
Whence the courage to come to you, my friend,
For my motive was amorous in the end,

And that love gave me the power to bend
The bars of my self-made cage and escape.
Nothing required you to reciprocate

For the gift of your texts had already reshaped
The geography of my mental landscape,
And that was more than enough to justify

Friendship, even if it came from just one side."
"And yet," he said, "even before I died,
You began to look elsewhere and found Badiou,

Comedy, Book Three

Whose ontology strangely appealed to you,
Though his mathematical reason perhaps
Posited yet another metaphysical trap,

Another groundless ground, another lapse
Into the dream of foundationalism,
Though I admit there may have been wisdom

In using the mathematical prism
To fracture being into its infinite parts
Minus the One that incorporates and imparts

To the whole the absolute origin that starts
The ball rolling, but his own great abstraction—
Though he sees it as a power of subtraction

Of categories that hide the main attraction,
Not God above but the empty set that contains
Infinite possibilities in what remains

The uncountable multiplicity that sustains
The concrete appearance of the multitude—
Such an abstraction could easily delude

The mind into projecting another skewed
Dogmatism that mistakes posited axioms
For concrete absolutes that become reactions

Against truth as process when they lead to actions
That lose track of the unbounded context
And responsibility that cannot rest

While time puts each decision to the test."

CANTO 23

"Responsibility without closure,"
I then spoke up, "is the ethical cynosure,
The guiding star that forces the exposure

Of what exceeds the appearance of foreclosure,
Whether reading a text or writing a law,
For constitutions should not be held in awe

As if the authors who wrote them foresaw
All the twists and turns of perpetual drift
Of context insaturable where each rift

That seems like negation becomes a gift,
The opening to the other somehow missed,
Which responsibility cannot resist

But sends the invitation to exist
And join the reformation that persists
With the knowledge that the universal call

Is not exclusive but addressed to all,
For subtraction of categories leaves space
Immeasurable like a *khôra* or place

Before placement, but one of infinite grace
Where everything possible to write is written,
Where every difference find its recognition,

And every bond of love has its position
Without exclusion clauses—where every race,
Face, trace, embrace is no longer debased

By the fantasies of those who would erase
The fullness of being that survives the lies
And haunts every present with a surprise,

The something in excess that never dies.
John Lennon wrote, *Imagine there's no heaven*,
And *All you need is love* as yeast to leaven

Comedy, Book Three

The human spirit and remove the leaden
Weight that keeps the imagination down
With ghostly categories that keep us bound

To the dream of what's above when on the ground
The paradise of multitude abounds,
Where love is militant cooperation

That breaks through borders through creative negation,
And if perception itself phantomalizes,
As you seem to have said—is that a crisis?

If everything's a ghost, the ghost comprises
Its own negation when it imagines the real
As the resistance to every ideal,

Because love is more than just what we feel
But thought as process that speaks through action,
For they are one, not reflection or reaction

But materialization of abstraction,
Forcing the existence of a living phantom.
For isn't thought itself the ghost that haunts

Interminably our passions and wants,
Forcing us to question every decision
With the responsibility of revision

If the truth process requires a change of position.
You are such a ghost who haunts this waking dream,
And I've not been faithful to what may seem

Your right of response that might wish to undream
Unintended misreadings that must teem
In my words that mix yours with those of Badiou,

Lacan, and others, including your friend Bourdieu,
For you questioned the Marxist concept of class
As fused consciousness with the power to blast

Canto 23

Bourgeois order to kingdom come at last,
While Bourdieu saw class struggle as diffuse relations,
Spurred not by identity but situations

Through trajectories of endless variations,
And for me this was another revelation."
Then Derrida to me: "You needn't waste

Your time apologizing that the trace
I am combines and configures in different shapes
With other traces in your head that call

Out to you and me like that of Stendhal.
Le Rouge et le Noir, The Red and the Black—the fall
Of Julien Sorel may be like a blueprint,

Mapping the history of your resentment,
But could it also be my own history?
For those who know me know there's no mystery

About my addiction to love that incredibly
Was the flip side of my marginality,
The continuous haunting of *nostalgérie*,

The Algeria living on the inner me,
The heart of my carefully nurtured secrecy,
For like Julien my place was out of place,

Though never just my sense of class or race,
But I felt the need to keep a constant pace
To stay ahead of enemies and lovers

And lovers can be enemies undercover,
For when Julien loved he loved a phantom,
Though the object of his projection was not random,

But the class with which he dreamed he would become
One by possessing the icon of wealth, woman,
That most private property—and my love too

Comedy, Book Three

Conjured up ghosts in a supplemental coup
To force admission of this Algerian Jew
To the kingdom of sameness, even though I knew

It was a wasteland in which nothing grew.
But Julien finally saw Madame de Rênal
Not as a thing possessed but as one whose fall

Was an ascension from every banal
Relation, for she alone had given her all,
And only when death took command of his life

Could he release himself from constant strife,
And like Emma Bovary on the day she dies,
See the love never seen before in the eyes

Of one who was the antithesis of lies.
Though I was driven to seek love everywhere,
There was only one who laid her heart bare,

Though it irks me to use words so utterly unrare."
"Class relations," I said, "can give rise to perverse
Passion when the attraction of the adverse—

Even though the love is real—becomes a curse
Because the contradictions of habitus,
Or how class-inflected cultures conceive us,

Can lead to unintended betrayals of trust.
As a young man, I read Stendhal and there saw
An image of *ressentiment* in awe

Of things out of reach that constantly gnaw
On consciousness until all it can see
Is the lack, and that way a void comes to be

The idea of heaven, and that was me,
But unlike Julien I never doubted the truth
Of love, even when it felt like abuse,

Canto 23

Because no passion ever fails to induce
A greater power of love that passes on
To another and another and beyond

Until it finds a heart that can respond.
Then what seemed a curse seems like nothing worse
Than a bend in the road that forced one to rehearse

For the work of love and its constant rebirths,
For love changes and is never the same,
But one person can justify the chain

And redeem all the loves whose traces remain.
Class contradictions infiltrate every emotion—
Every relation that commands devotion

Can quickly undergo a demotion,
So that love becomes hate and hate a seduction
That inadvertently leads to its own deconstruction

To become a love that exceeds dyadic reduction.
Class struggle should not be the will to destroy
But to expand the social bond and deploy

All the powers of everyone to enjoy
A greater existence, for the love of two
Transcends itself like Joyce's *seim anew*

To become the love of all the multitude.
No real love, even when it is betrayed,
Is ever a loss in some uneven trade

But steps forward in a process that must be weighed
Against the dream of a common existence."
"But what if your final love becomes past tense?"

Said Derrida, and then I: "The only defense
Against loss is infinite love that never
Lets go even when no longer together

Comedy, Book Three

Lovers cannot see each other ever,
Like the love of God in a novel Graham Greene wrote.
Though God may not exist that name connotes

Love as thought that can never be revoked."

CANTO 24

Derrida then spoke: "Go on now, living on,
   At least for a while, as you reflect upon
  Class struggle as love that can never be won

Through violence or the murder of anyone,
  Though love may require acts of self-sacrifice,
   Because human beings succumb to lies

And their blindness should never be a surprise
  As it projects phantoms that create divides
   That keep the multitude at war with itself,

Since some have none and others all the wealth."
  Though infinitely more could have been said,
   This living phantom joined the other dead

Who go on living in each and every head
Where their consciousness survives and is still read
  As thoughts encased in words that come in waves

And spread out from the signatory phrase
  Shadowy influences that forget the name
But the thought process carries on just the same,

For no one dies without traces that remain.
  When I walked out the gate on the Rue d'Ulm,
   My mind went dark until it awoke in a room

And I didn't know where I was or what to assume
When a young woman entered who seemed quite vexed
  But familiar, which left me feeling perplexed,

When she looked at me and said, "Ah, he recollects
Nothing of the one who challenged him years ago
  In this room, when I complained that he would show

That movie by John Ford that felt like a blow
  Against my people, though you didn't know
   I was an indigenous woman in your class

Comedy, Book Three

Who feared my words to you might just get laughs,
    Because Oklahoma was new to you and I
  Didn't think you'd fathom the reason why

  Someone like me would see the film as a lie.
    But your face right now can be easily read—
  Now that you recall me, you think I'm dead,

  But I'm only a reflection in your head,
    Where I've been living on, a separate life,
  And you'll never know what the other was like,

  But let's just say, I had the will to fight,
    And never stayed silent about what's right,
    Having descended from a warrior clan,

  And frankly feeling as strong as any man."
    "OU was the place where I began my career,"
Was my response, "and though I found friends here,

  Who gave me the confidence to persevere,
  I looked to the future with some degree of fear,
    And when you came to this office that day,

    I was disturbed by what you had to say,
  And though I didn't think I'd committed a sin,
I admired your courage because you spoke out when

  You saw something wrong, but I had to defend
  My decision to teach John Ford's masterpiece,
  But not to argue for innocence that bespeaks

  Some universal truth that escapes critiques
    But rather to expose contradictions
  That derive consciously or not from afflictions

  That cannot be erased by canonical ascriptions.
    The word 'Masterpiece' lacks universal
  Address because it can never speak for all

Canto 24

The multitude in its subjective call
To witness aesthetic value, but something true
In the ugly face of oppression can still shine through—

And against the lies that made you feel so blue,
Ford's indictment of the American myth
And the racism of his hero made short shrift

Of his own past constructions and created a rift
In the Western's ideological monolith.
But the door Ford opened he quickly slammed shut,

And if John Wayne was shut out, the deeper cut
Against history was Ford's failure to redeem
Contradictions by showing that what may seem

Like a harmless image has power to demean
More than the cultural past but the present
Consciousness, and even art that seeks divestment

Of history's nightmare by exposing repellent
Truth does not fully transcend implication
In the horror of its imperfect evocation

Of the violence that gave birth to a nation.
Art's redemption is the careful dissection
Of the different layers of its inflection

Of the past to give ground to the correction,
Not of events that cannot be undone
But of the future that we must will to come

Through words and acts that speak to everyone."
Then she: "You're right, some things can't be undone.
For my people, the story of Oklahoma

Is like the excision of a carcinoma,
Only we were the tumor that got cut out
And cast aside while forcing us to doubt

Comedy, Book Three

Our own culture, which they tried to put to rout.
But if we were the cancer on the white nation,
Our violence was no aberration—

We learned cruelty through the observation
Of the Spanish and then your pale ancestors,
Whom we fought and became the terror of the settlers,

Who were never innocent but the abettors
Of our annihilation—we who had
Ruled the plains and taught Apaches how bad

We could be, but that story makes me sad,
For if all our forces had come together,
Who knows what we might have done and whether

Our story might not have been tragically tethered
To yours, until we became the afterthought
Of U.S. history in which we were caught

Like in a spiderweb, the threads of a plot
To force us into the religion of property,
Which to us too often only meant poverty

When white men engaged in legal robbery,
Which seemed the true expression of their faith.
The Osage people decided to embrace

Property as a way to secure their people's place
After the allotment travesty took away
The false promise of forever and a day,

And their underground reservation could pay,
From barrels of oil according to each headright,
Enough wealth to make them believe the fight

For survival in the culture of the white
Was over, but then the crooked guardians came
And once again white men decided to tame

Canto 24

The wild Indians who might use their wealth to claim
  Equality with the White Race and the laws
Were on the side of corruption which soon caused

White men to marry women they called 'squaws'
  Among themselves and love was trumped by greed,
    Which in the white psyche is like a weed

That grows and covers every vital seed
  Until it rots the love that might have been,
    For even some who loved were quick to sin

Until murderous love was in the wind
That blew through the Osage nation like a gas,
Poisonous and mind-numbing that led at last

To another genocide or killing *en masse*,
  For who can count just how many had died
    From poison, for the numbers never lied,

Too many in their prime—it can't be denied.
White people in Oklahoma thought no more
Of killing us in nineteen-twenty-four

Than in any of the years that came before.
  A few got justice but most got away.
    That's how it was—sometimes still is today.

So I mean no disrespect to you when I say,
  Theories like yours may just rationalize
    The irreversible loss our waking eyes

Never stop seeing behind your national lies.
  I cannot forgive, though I am no Osage
    And my people fought them back in the days

When enemies could respect each other's ways,
But killing people for money like those black folk
In Tulsa were killed because their wealth awoke

Comedy, Book Three

Envy and fear in white men who were broke
Or broken by other white men who took all
The wealth for themselves and used race as a wall

Built in the mind with the purpose to enthrall
Poor whites to the only god they can truly call
Their own—for money they will never betray,

Like they do Jesus when he gets in the way—
Yes, killing for money does not deserve respect.
When you came here to teach, what did you expect?

Oklahoma's history is a train wreck."

CANTO 25

"Oklahoma's history is the history
Of this country," I said, "but your story
Projected a gaze that never looked away

And knew what art reveals it can betray,
But that contradiction is the signature
Of truth that solicits a countersignature

In the voice that calls out the caricature
Of what the imagination fails to perceive,
For popular art can never fail to leave

Some blind spot that warrants no other reprieve
Than full exposure of what it would misconceive—
But doesn't all art strive to be popular?

For what lies behind the myth of the author
Is the voice of the multitude that occupies
The singular mind from which nothing can arise

That does not in some way economize
On the polyphonic essence of all art,
Which means no work of art is whole but a part

That escapes from the brain like from a sieve and carts
The partial truth with traces of what's left out,
Sometimes unknown to the artists themselves who doubt

What others see as if it were the shroud
Of Turin, but the truth of art is not
In the work alone but like a borromean knot,

Through interlinked connections that never stop,
It spreads out through a temporal procedure
That generates truthful points that configure

Into a shape that reveals what would disfigure
Truth's infinite address without closure,
For the false projects a finite cover to hide

Comedy, Book Three

What cannot be measured and then divides
The multitude against itself through exclusion
Of the universal that either means inclusion

Or becomes a simulacrum through occlusion.
To call any one culture universal
And measure all others by this external

Standard makes the universal infernal,
The absolute betrayal of its concept,
Which over time creates a cultural debt

And not just for all the promises not kept.
A film entitled *Werk ohne Autor*—
In English you'd say *Work without Author*,

But *Never Look Away* was the title that bore
The political dimension of its truth—
Is like a Bildungsroman a story of youth.

A boy, whose aunt's passion for art eschews
Nazis who hate art as a political ruse,
Learns from her the force of the aesthetic gaze

That has the power to set the world ablaze,
Not with fire but the beauty in all things,
But for her the possession of this vision brings

The verdict of madness from those without the wings
To soar above a world where nothing is seen
That does not conform to the colorless routine

Of a daily life where difference is obscene—
(Yes, this echoes for me in a personal way,
Because for some my mother was just the cliché

Of someone insane whose mind had gone astray,
But she was the first to instill in me theory
Or the intellectual power of reverie

Canto 25

That unearths possibilities others bury,
And she never looked away from good or bad,
Which sometimes made her sad and others mad

Who feared the truth her witness revealed that had
Parallels with what the boy's aunt deplored)—
So the Nazis had her case referred to a board

Of doctors who used eugenics like a sword,
And among them was one whom she so annoyed
It made him sentence her to be destroyed,

But the look from her the boy could not avoid
Was when they dragged her away and he raised his hand
To cover the eye from horrors it can't stand

Like a filter that enables it to withstand
Deadly truth—and he lowered and raised and lowered
The hand, not to be blinded by what he abhorred,

Like gazing into a black sun that can score
The eye with traces burned into the brain,
And though the boy forgot, something remained

And was reborn in the artist he became.
Then the passionate love of a woman led him back
To the medical monster who used his skills to attack

Whatever didn't fit into the pack
Of the Aryan white race when euthanasia
Was the name of the effort to create a

Master race in which the doctor played a
Leading role—(and if my mother had lived
There and then nothing would make me forgive

Those who would take away her right to live
Because her vision could see through the lies
That men without imagination devise

And plug their ears so they don't hear the cries
Of the beauty they destroy because they despise
Whatever falls outside of their program)—

But though the artist did not know the sham
Practice that lay behind the doctor's mask
Of respectability, it became the task

Of his art to dig into the unconscious past
Archived in memory and resurrected
By old photos in which he detected

A truth he had not known or suspected,
So he put the face of the young woman, his aunt,
With the face of the doctor who never could recant

The crime's monstrosity for which he can't
Take responsibility until he sees
The truth in art that causes him to freeze

With a recognition nothing can appease,
And though he does not die, he's dead inside,
And from the aesthetic gaze he cannot hide,

But the artist looks on without pleasure or pride
Because he doesn't know the reason why
This man suddenly walks away in a daze,

And that may be the meaning of the phrase,
'Work without Author' because we do not know
All the voices that live in our heads and bestow

On us like seeds truths that get watered and grow
Through experiences we think we dissect
All on our own, but art has its own project

That may exceed intentions and connect
Unconsciously to something we feel but don't see."
And then she: "How does all this apply to me?

Canto 25

Am I an artist? Is all the world Germany?"
"Artist or not, you are a beautiful soul,"
I replied, "because you confronted me with the role

I played in fostering blindness to the toll
Aesthetic lies can take on people's lives,
And it made me look at my teaching and revise

What I should say in order to emphasize
The contradictions apparent to your eyes,
But more importantly your thought survives

In me to this day as a voice to analyze
The subtle ways in which I look away,
Which may not have been at all what you meant to say,

But it's a constant warning not to betray
Out of ignorance the multitudes in my head
That only have the appearance of being dead

For their common thought is a continuous thread,
And though it can be frayed and cut and lost,
It will resurrect itself without loss

To a becoming that time cannot exhaust."
"Never look away, okay, but the hand
Sometimes rises because no one can stand

To look on history's cruelty without some strand
Of hope, and I know we'll never get back the land,
But I have to believe a reckoning will come."

She spoke and was gone, and I heard a deafening humm
Like a swarm of bees or locusts and something ate
The space around me that left me in a state

Of free fall until I seemed to gyrate
And I thought I was about to disintegrate
When I felt the ground and then heat all around

And found myself sitting atop a mound.

CANTO 26

I looked down and saw two men on the ground,
And they were two who on occasion had frowned
On my blunt tongue when we were all colleagues—

For I was not one for quiet intrigues
But direct confrontation was my default
Practice, which some saw as direct assault

On their expertise and therefore such a fault
That made friendships most difficult to sustain—
But now both had crossed over to a domain

That some call heaven but I call the brain
In the collective sense of a human chain
Of mental fibers that through constant exchange

Of memories combine and rearrange
Into a greater human form like Blake's
Jesus or Joyce's Finnegans who wake

From the final sleep of the flesh and then partake
In the infinite thought that binds the multitude,
All the living and all the dead imbued

Each with some fragment of the infinite truth.
So I climbed down and stood before the two,
One who long since had passed but the other was new

To the world of the dead, which made so many blue,
For he was loved in a way only a few
Souls experience, and I wondered if he knew.

Then to them both I said, "I saw LSU
Sometimes as a prisonhouse with no exit,
Louisiana Shawshank—that says it—

A phrase I sometimes used—I confess it—
Which annoyed some who saw my negative jest
As ingratitude for the way I had been blessed

Canto 26

With a career those who are truly oppressed
Can only dream of, but behind the critique
I constantly expressed was the unique

Joy I took in the freedom that let me speak
The things I took as truths life had imposed
On me, self-evident like those proposed

By old Jefferson, though he was not disposed
To follow the infinite track of his axiom,
For the truth process has no perfect medium

And can be lost in the daily tedium
That clouds the mind with a swarm of opinions."
Then the elder John replied, "All men are equal—

For you there was no qualifying sequel
To limit equality to some prequel,
As if it only applies to the fetal,

Or only to the good and not the evil,
For fall and redemption, betrayal and repentance,
That's the life process itself without transcendence,

And though some turn life into a death sentence
And leave a legacy of blind vengeance,
They are still a part of the human form divine

Like a foil that reflects and intensifies the shine
Of truth, and it's our duty to redeem,
Not the evil itself, but the source that may seem

Inhuman, and when sometimes the failure foreseen
Sways us toward the negation we oppose,
It's our own righteousness we must expose

To the light of critical consciousness that knows
How the evil we see covers the evil we are.
I once betrayed myself in a scene bizarre

Comedy, Book Three

When I joined the mob in calling to the bar
Of our kangaroo court one whose only sin
Was trusting a superior who had been

Negligent about when things begin and end,
But I chose power over the powerless
Because I thought I was judicious and blessed

With deductive powers that might have impressed
Sherlock Holmes or Oliver Wendel no less—
And then I thought I'd straighten you out in time

But instead you called me out for a thoughtless crime,
Which I ignored until some years had passed
And I found it hard to live with that past,

A memory that came to seem more and more crass.
So I had to ask myself, was I evil?
Was my righteous authority lethal?

How badly did I harm innocent people?"
To which I replied: "John, please don't misconstrue
My thought, for as I later learned from Badiou,

Evil itself must be a relation to truth,
But negative in the different ways it betrays
The truth process, sometimes through a malaise

That darkens our days and causes us to raise
The flag of surrender, or when we seek to please
Others or defend some dreamed-of expertise

That issues its opinions as decrees
Without exceptions—oh, evil has its degrees,
But the worse is to destroy truth's own being

Through dogma and simulacra that murder seeing
Or murder human beings we stigmatize
By creating a false universal that lies

Canto 26

When we imagine evil as what abides
Elsewhere or anywhere but in ourselves,
But though in each of us some evil dwells,

Communal power is the fuel that propels
It like a rocket toward some imagined target,
Someone who gets dragged onto the docket

Because they awakened something asleep in the closet.
John, the evil in you is the same in me
But I can only hope that there might be

As much good in me as in you I see.
You were the only one who admitted some wrong,
And who can say they've never gone along

With some betrayal for fear they might be drawn
Into the circle of those who don't belong.
Belonging may be a natural human desire

Unless exclusion makes it a razor wire
That cuts in both directions and wounds us all
Because it kills the universal call

Of common existence to knock down every wall."
Then John: "I have watched your dream unfold on the screen
In your head and witnessed with sadness the scene

Of his return, I mean the one I'd seen
As culpable, and dangerous for you,
And that he died young now makes me feel blue,

Though where I live today I see him too
And rejoice knowing I did not kill his passion
For life—and hope I learned more compassion,

Which had been blinded by false dispassion."
"John," I said, "errors were made on every side,
But the true culprit was the one who lied,

And allowed collective delusions to preside
Over the moral consciousness that pride
Had taken possession of, and he could've stopped

The lunacy but instead like Iago propped
It up, but his true motive may never be known,
Though I knew him to be a man most prone

To falsehood, and I was not the only one."
Then the other whose name was also John spoke out:
"I was stunned to learn what this was all about,

Why people of color were being put to rout,
For there was more than one and the black woman
Was my friend and we had a field in common,

But I did not speak out as loudly as some
And was shaken when you pulled out the big gun
And fired the word 'racism' at everyone,

Which seemed risky since my tenure was yet to come,
While you knew yours was practically in hand—
So I wasn't quite ready to join your band

For fear it might leave a permanent brand.
Besides, I didn't trust your stability,
Your mother having died quite recently,

And also I knew you didn't care for me."
"John," I replied, "over the years you said
That to me many times, but the place in my head

You occupy says something else instead.
Though I sought your friendship, it never came,
But looking back, it seems we're both to blame.

I was estranged from the academic domain,
Which I saw as class-ridden and proclaimed
It in ways that made others think I blamed

Canto 26

    Their successes for the evils I had named
        In what I saw as a zero-sum game.
    I don't believe that was completely false,

But right or wrong, in the end it was my loss."

CANTO 27

"You and I together once took a shot
At curriculum that blindly ignored the lot
Of all the peoples history had forgot,

And for once we caused the system to adopt
A change that might have seemed like a ripple then,
But which created waves that would extend

Beyond our awareness of how it had to begin—
And at that time I would have called you friend."
So spoke the younger John and I replied:

"Looking back in time after you had died,
I remembered that occasion with some pride,
But we were not always on the same side

And that caused us to let the friendship slide—
Still if I was a challenge to my friends
When we seemed to pursue different ends,

And if too often I was one who offends
With passionate opposition that ignored
The authority of expertise that scored

So high among the academic horde,
It was not for lack of respect or even affection,
But I came to it from a different direction,

Never having known prestigious selection—
And yes, there was resentment like a fire
I sought to contain before it burned the fiber

Of love, which while making me a fighter
Did not make me negate the contrary,
Because if I made everyone wary

Of a passion they feared one day might miscarry,
I also feared the same and knew the blame
To myself, by myself, would be ascribed and stain

Canto 27

The truth process I struggled to sustain.
One name for that process is equality,
But with a meaning beyond ideology

That makes each individual a commodity
Harvested for some political endeavor,
When to be equal is to be beyond measure,

Not something to be gathered up like treasure,
A *vox populi* under the thumb of someone
Who transforms a collective voice into a gun

To shoot down what democracy has won.
Every law or principle that seeks to define
Equality produces another blind

That must be addressed or it will undermine
A process without closure in finite time.
The same can be said for freedom and justice,

Truth processes that are endlessly restless,
For no proposition can tame their force
To generate new directions in their course,

And the word 'communism' that some would divorce
From these others is intertwined with them
Or it has been betrayed—that's why I condemn

What communist ideology has been
In states that use it to disempower
The multitude who are made to cower

Before dictators who take from them their hour
And turn back the clock to the old nightmare."
Then the second John: "You're way up in the air

From anything about which I could care.
I just wanted to teach and nurture voices
Of people who had been denied the choices

Comedy, Book Three

    I had, while you imitated Joyce's
Path of writing what no one can understand.
    I answered to a minority demand

For careers that would enable them to expand
The story of cultures and histories left untold,
    And forgive me if you think I am too bold,

    But is it bragging to sit back and behold
The generations of young scholars I'd call
    My intellectual progeny who all

Have advanced a cause no reaction can appall?
I know they'll stand up to those who have tried,
Like that fool in Florida who before I died

Sought to erase history with a law that lied
    About the nature of historical truth
And even accused us of corrupting youth—

    I believe my teaching will be put to use
By those who aren't afraid to sing the blues.
    Even scholarship is a kind of art

That sometimes gives expression to the heart,
And you can see how many mine has touched,
But like for any bluesman whose hand has struck

    Down a major chord it wasn't all luck
And dark corners of my soul couldn't stay hidden
But found expression in the things I'd written,

Like this mound whose message to us remains unbidden
    But stands here as testimony to a past
That no matter how hard we may try to cast

    It aside—like these students who have passed
It by, not knowing what it might signify—
    It rises up in our path and will survive

Canto 27

To force the truth that the WAS of time is alive.
African Americans and Caribbeans
I served in my work, not the Europeans,

For the universal exceeds the Shakespearean
And that was the only theory I needed,
Which you ultimately may have conceded,

Though I felt you thought I had not succeeded
In theoretical sophistication."
"John," I answered back, "I take this oration,

And your allusion to a First Nation,
As self-evident in the sense that your axiom
Lies embedded in your application,

A political act without reservation
That shows devotion to human liberation.
I never questioned the value of your work

And both of us on occasion went beserk
With the vanity academia inspires,
But neither of us ever surrendered the higher

Purpose of our work, which is not to find a buyer,
But to take small steps toward revelation
Of the power of human imagination

To create conditions for social transformation,
And though in isolation those steps are small,
The intellectual labor of us all

Broadcasts to the world an unequivocal call
To join the chorus of the universal
Comedy, which may not lead to a reversal

Of all evil but to something just as eternal,
A becoming like an infinite rehearsal
That discovers in itself the true ending

Comedy, Book Three

In a commitment to truth unrelenting.
But along the way we're blessed with little heavens,
Which for me took the form of amorous lessons

From lovers and friends who laughed at my depressions
And taught me to feel eternity in a kiss,
And for you that and something so many miss,

A heaven of friendships that fills the abyss
Of human desire with a love never remiss.
So few of us are loved by as many as you,

And that's a legacy you had to accrue
Through gifts of grace that cannot be measured."
Then the elder John: "I wouldn't have conjectured

A moment like this, though I often lectured
One of you on the necessity to forgive,
Without which it's impossible to live

With other human beings who don't give
The answer you expect or want or need,
But this much both of you will have to concede,

You don't have to be a hero to plant a seed,
And small acts can add up to something greater
Than we expect, through effects that come much later,

After the mortal body has turned traitor
To consciousness and we depend on the lives
Of others, on their brains in which survives

Some trace of us not even recognized
That flows into an ocean without shores.
But rising up from time's volcanic stores

Come islands of consciousness that are nothing more
Than stations where we pause and catch our breaths,
For the crossing is measured by multiple deaths—

And resurrections that make a life that's blessed."

CANTO 28

The two Johns walked away, so up the mound
I climbed, feeling lost as I sat back down,
But suddenly on the screen in my head came round

The projection of a scene that had seemed profound
To me once, with the music of Jackson Browne—
The song "Late for the Sky"—in the background,

And the person captivated by that sound,
Coming from his TV, was De Niro's
Character in *Taxi Driver*, not a hero,

But someone who had reached the degree zero
Of human belonging, and I don't know why,
But that broken man's face made me want to cry,

For I felt myself always late for the sky
And the man's loneliness was like a shroud
That covers the whole human species that's bowed

And broken because it misses its avowed
Heaven, and nostalgia for paradise lost
Gives birth to political sects and desires crisscrossed

Until happiness is a dream that comes at a cost
Only a few can afford, and they live in
Fear of the masses who won't forgive them—

So in the end nothing's left to believe in.
But while I sat there feeling so lonely,
A woman climbed up who once had known me,

And how could I be surprised when only
Memorable souls followed me in this dream?
She said, "Sitting or walking here may seem

Disrespectful of a place we should esteem
If buried here are the dead of a First Nation,
So rise up and we'll fly to a better location."

Comedy, Book Three

We both stood and by force of her inspiration
Rose into the sky and flew toward the West
Until we came to a green place that felt blessed,

And she said, "This is Blake's Beulah, a place of rest,
And though like me it only exists in your head,
It is the real mental cure of your dread,

When you feel lost in the shadows of the dead."
Then I: "Sylviane, I have long mourned your fate
And the violence I discovered too late

That haunted your life when love turned into hate."
Then she: "Sit down on this green grass and breathe
The air of militant compassion unsheathed

Against the cult of vengeance that's bequeathed
To generations by histories like my own.
On the horror of genocide I had shone

A bright light, but then that history came home
When love unexpectedly became murder
And everyone thought, 'He would never hurt her,'

But injustice breeds rage, the great perverter,
And even I could not believe evil
Could make a heart once loved into a lethal

Weapon that attacked my soul like some primeval
God at war with the eternal feminine,
And when he could not conquer my sentiment,

He chose to turn me into a revenant,
And I lost my beautiful Angelina.
Knowing his cruel love, I should have foreseen a

Violent act when I said I'd take his *niña*,
But I knew one day his uncontrollable rage
Would turn on this innocent when she was an age

Canto 28

Where he no longer was master of the stage
And she no longer spoke the lines he writes—
So I imagined some horrifying nights

But never dreamed his rage could reach such heights
That he would murder me and I cannot say
What he did in the night before he ran away

With my daughter—and how could he betray
My love for her by covering with lies
The missing grave in which my memory lies?

But a mother's love is a force that never dies
And love like life finds a way to survive,
Because even in his head I'm still alive

And in his lonely cell he will revive
The love he murdered and forever lost.
I'm glad the death penalty is not his cross

For that would've been for me another loss,
For such a vengeance could never appease
My broken heart that has found its own peace

In forgiveness, which does not mean I will cease
To cast a critical gaze at human horror
And for my daughter wish I could stand before her

And shield her from monsters who might destroy her,
But then I remember something you said to me—
Believing in a god you cannot see

Is not the hardest faith, which has to be
Belief in the goodness of the human race
Despite the monstrosities that have laid waste

To hope, desire, and love, and every grace
That ennobles the human spirit—that's the faith
Required to move mountains because it strives

Comedy, Book Three

To see beyond death to the truth that survives,
And now my purpose here is to revive
Your faith, and let me for once be your teacher

And remind you that in every human creature,
Though evil exists, so does the generous heart,
And evil mostly derives from a bad start

When human cruelty leaves its deadly mark
On the innocent soul that then construes the gift
Of love as a threat that may leave them adrift

And that which should have joined creates a rift
That allows fear and jealousy to flood the mind
Until all tenderness is left behind."

"Sylviane, your visitation is just in time,"
I said, "for I feel the end of my vision near,
And suddenly am filled with a strange fear,

Which may explain why I've summoned you here.
In my head I see so many souls I've known—
Whose memories in my brain live and have grown

Into something more than what was first sown
By their living presence—but they failed to achieve
The realization of a dream they believed

Explained the reason why they were conceived.
Some wanted fame, some wanted love, and some
Wanted money, or maybe just to become

More than they were in the places they came from—
But does anyone ever reach paradise,
Aside from fantasies of the afterlife?

Why are we never satisfied and strive
Always for something further down the road
Until we die and others bear the load

Canto 28

Of our secret despair that has overflowed
Into their lives like a chain reaction—
Like Mick Jagger sang, no satisfaction

Ever comes, but instead a subtraction
Of the will to live when fame wanders away,
Or money only buys you mental decay,

Or love only creates the desire to betray.
But then I think of you, and though the worst
Happened to you that some would call a curse,

I remember the joy in your face when you gave birth
To the one who for you always had to come first."
Then she: "My death and others' may seem unfair,

While violent histories can conjure despair,
And sometimes we descend into that old slough,
But lingering there isn't worthy of you,

Knowing that the only value of feeling blue
Is to rise up and use it to renew
The passion for life that death can't extinguish

Because paradise is not the end but the wish
To begin again in the fullness of being,
Which embraces all of time without leaving

Behind anyone's mental conceiving,
And thoughts you transferred to me I transfer back
To you to keep them on the infinite track

That cannot be obstructed by any lack.
Think of the dark violence of Scorsese's
Cinema, and how it would be so easy

To see goodness as the trick of some Houdini,
But instead from those films you take inspiration
And experience a kind of joyous elation

In the presence of passionate imagination."

CANTO 29

"You're right, life at the movies was my heaven,
Not filled with angels and saints, holy brethren
Who take human souls to knead and leaven

Until they rise and join that most reverend
Crew who feed the light of Dante's white rose—
No, in my heaven only flawed heroes

Sometimes rise up and against the odds oppose
The very evil they themselves once chose
Either to follow or to look away—

And yes, in this creation Scorsese's sway—
For me—is unparalleled since I saw
That look on De Niro's face and felt with awe

The man behind the camera who could draw
Out of it images that showed Christ-like
Compassion for the darkest souls who might

Be saved if someone had the will to fight
To bring them out of darkness into the light.
He forced me to see the depths of human cruelty

In the dark history of his own great city—
Or the violence of wild masculinity—
Or women trapped in the web of misogyny—

Or monsters bred from swamps of poverty
As the waste products of privileged community—
Or the power of capital to create and destroy

What it creates using as the standard ploy
The right to wealth that only those enjoy
Who nonchalantly take what others make

And either ignore the law or legislate
The right to steal when they incorporate.
But sometimes even his killers can be saints

Canto 29

And aristocrats gangsters without restraints.
The madness of broken love can force the hand,
"To live as a monster or die as a good man"—

But in the mission of priests in old Japan,
One man dies and the other betrays his faith,
But while the goal of both men is to save,

The one who sacrifices sainthood gave
The harder lesson in imitation of Christ.
Even Jesus had to struggle against the vice

Of self-righteousness that thought itself all-wise
Until he came to the garden of absent joys
Where he was forced to make the ethical choice

Between life and death without hearing the voice
Of divine certainty, because Kazantzakis
And Scorsese knew, the meaning of Judas's kiss

Is the knowledge that only human flesh can resist
The submission of human spirit to Roman
Conquest, even in the guise of a showman

Who hypnotizes the crowd like a Trojan
Horse that carries inside not the hidden
Enemy but the darkness that comes unbidden

Out of the multitude itself when driven
To a frenzy of self-hate and self-deception.
Scorsese forces the visual perception

Of Marx's own historical conception—
When tragedy repeats itself, it's farce—
And no one on the left can better parse

The contradictions of capital's sparse
Ethical foundations than the comic inferno
Of that cathedral of cash called a casino

Comedy, Book Three

Where desert digs make the *contrapasso,*
While Wall Street wolves with insane mediocrity,
Teeth dripping with the blood of democracy,

Sing drunken hosannas to their plutocracy,
And the tragedy of organized labor,
When they create and then kill their savior,

Are the strings manipulated by their slaver,
And the love that should have been their sacred bond
Becomes a cover to hide the master's con

Until the time to act has come and gone.
That song that speaks of Jesus's 'doubt and pain'
And all the cops criminals and sinners saints

Sums up Scorsese's cinema and explains
Why the Rolling Stones join on the soundtrack
Of his world where every door seems painted black.

But against a background that spells out the lack
Of compassion appear the Dalai Lama
And Méliès, the father of dream cinema—

The saint and the artist who give us a vision of
A world where dreams belong to everyone,
Not the world we're told is the only one

Whose historical symbols are the whip and the gun—
Since despite the will to conquer and control
The collective mind, no one can own the soul

Of multitude because the infinite whole
Imprints itself on every finite part,
The appearance of which is the essence of art,

And from somewhere always comes a new start."
Then Sylviane: "You know I chose to write
On traumatic histories that were a blight

Canto 29

On human existence, and yet my vision was bright,
   My essence never sadness but delight,
  And I chose you as guide because your passion

    For truth enabled me to imagine
  That knowledge of horror was not negation
    But a necessary investigation,

  Prelude to what must be the restoration
  Of human hope through secular revelation,
And my life's meaning should not lie in my death

   As if with my body gone nothing is left
   Of me, because nobody is one body,
And as long as there are brains there's somebody

    Who links our being to everybody—
  No thought that approaches truth is ever lost,
  No human essence ever dies on the cross,

  The life process has no exclusion clause—
  Even where consciousness seems not to exist,
   There's a force in matter that will persist,

  And against every lie being itself resists.
 Those people who lived through the Holocaust
    Had to discover at a terrible cost

The meaning of not-one when their lives were crossed
  Not just by others but themselves as the other—
 When the nightmare of the one who had to suffer

   Loss of world became another cover
  That hid the innocence that came before
From the one who survived and had to close the door

   On the other two and on so many more—
  The self became multiple and selves combined
 Exposed the crack in a world that was predefined

Comedy, Book Three

To which the survivor could be no longer blind.
This is the lesson I took from Charlotte Delbo
And in my death its truth must overflow

The boundaries of my life that won't forego
Resurrection in material existence
Where I inhabit minds through persistence

Of thought that is the ultimate resistance
To the evil that lies dormant in each of us.
The Bible says we come from dust and to dust

We return but in that dust I place my trust,
For as Philip Pullman understands that's where
Spirit and matter coincide like the air

We breathe but cannot see though it's still there.
We are dust through and through because we are spirit—
It's the same thing whether we admit it

Or not, but now I must conclude my visit.
Someone is coming whose love gave you a life,
A survivor of her own cruel mental strife,

And in this dream already before your eyes
She has appeared but in a cloak of sorrow,
But now she comes from a different tomorrow,

A time we no longer have to borrow,
Because it cannot be measured or contained.
Between us our friendship will always remain—

That's the other heaven time can't disdain.
If you see Angelina, tell her I'm there
Inside her where the eternity of my care

Folds her in the embrace of a mother's prayer."

CANTO 30

I saw her body fade into dust that shined
As if the light from each particle defined
A world to come—as many as stars in the sky,

Some greater, some worse—but I knew the reason why
She came into my world was to prophesy,
Not utopia or the fall, but the triumph

Of the good, not as the end but in defiance
Of evil's eternal recurrence that meets defeat
Repeatedly in the cycles of incomplete

Time from which the good can never retreat.
But then I heard a voice: "What is the good?"—
And it echoed in my head so that I could

Not fail to know the one who once had stood
Over me and protected me and who
Was my original teacher at the debut

Of my life, and now her prophecy came true
When I heard, "I promised to come back to you,"
And turned around to see my lost mother,

Who was young again in radiant color
As if some veil had been lifted from my eyes,
For though the clothes she wore were no surprise,

She glowed as if old age had been a disguise,
And the sorrow I had seen in her before
Had steeled itself to become a joy that bore

Something absolute I could not ignore,
Though I had no clue as to what it could be.
As I reached out and embraced her most tenderly,

She said, "As once you existed in me,
Now I in you find another existence,
But at first you saw only my repentance—

Comedy, Book Three

    Since I cannot undo the omittance
Of acts of love I wish I had performed,
  As I lay dying, that might have transformed

The bad memories of my daughters who mourned
  Not just my death but the feeling of betrayal
  That I should leave them before we could avail

    Ourselves of mutual forgiveness, a tale
Too often told between mothers and daughters,
    For too much love can poison the waters

  Of affection when mothers become plotters
    In the conspiracy to save their daughters
  From their mother's fate, but it was too late,

  And only time can now improve the state
    Of what we are—but my life's not double,
    Both sad and happy, nor is there trouble

    In paradise, for heaven's not a bubble
And the joys of existence continue just the same,
  Mixed with regrets for which we feel no shame,

  Because self-knowledge is our final domain,
Even if the self has become the life of others.
The heaven and hell religions teach are covers

  That blind us to our essence as true lovers—
    And what we love in each other is God,
    Which is not a bearded monster with a rod,

    Not a person, which is another facade,
  It's what we can't perceive but know is there,
  Like energy, like thought, like love, like air,

  But 'like' is wrong because it's everywhere
    And everything, call it the absolute,
But not as the unquestioned essence of truth—

Canto 30

No formulation of truth is beyond dispute.
Truth is absolute but not absoluteness,
Its becoming is its own goal, process

Infinite, infinitely incomplete no less,
It touches what it cannot name or define
But what it must continually refine

Along an interminable curving line.
Perhaps I don't express myself so well—
Limitations of the brain in which I dwell

Against our mutual thought sometimes rebel—
But when I ask what the good is, it's not
My game to tease the mind that has forgot

The direction of desire but to open the plot
To that infinite drift through which the thing persists
That we recognize only when it's missed,

Like failed revolutions whose truth consists
In forcing the negation of the track
That goes nowhere with the will to bring back

The purpose impetuous action sometimes lacked.
I told you I believe in God, but this
Is *amor Dei intellectualis*,

The intellectual love of God, which is
Beatitude in Spinoza's philosophy,
But if I spell God's name with a capital G,

With you I have no reason to disagree
If you prefer to say the totality
Of what is, or that line you used to say to me—

Not how things are but that they are we see—
That the world exists, that anything exists
Is the mystical, the miracle that enlists

Comedy, Book Three

Our wonder, our faith, to which all relativists
  Close their eyes and pretend it isn't there,
  Pretend no absolute demands our care—

All opinions are equal they say and despair.
  The good is what we know but cannot prove,
  Though it seizes our minds and makes us move,

Forcing us sometimes to break the groove—
  To think the impossible in search of the true."
  But Spinoza, Wittgenstein? Was this her voice?

Doubts stopped my ears like a deafening noise,
  And I stood there wavering over the choice
  To believe or not—had someone not-me spoken?

If so, was it a dream or had I awoken?
  "Though it may be a dream, you're not asleep,"
  She said, and I almost began to weep,

But I knew the time had come for me to speak.
  "You must know how I've struggled to write your name,
  How hard it has been for me ever to explain

What you were, what you are, what must forever remain
  Of you in me as if you'd never died.
  With my father, I could hold back the tide

Of emotion long enough as I stood by the side
  Of his death bed to contemplate what he was,
  To write the story of what a man does

Who cannot love himself or ever trust
  The love of others, a hate that overflows
  The bounds of self until the darkness grows

And consumes others' light like a blight on a rose.
  But your voice, your words, I can't summon or quote,
  I hear their echo and know what they evoked,

Canto 30

But can't document what drifts away remote
From exactitude, and I feel another loss."
Then she answered, "You should require no gloss,

My voice embedded in yours has not been lost.
Love that leaves the deepest mark in your heart
Cannot be forced out and then set apart,

For it has become one with the infinite part
That contains us both and touches the absolute—
The truth process to which we pay tribute

With different words to pave a common route.
If someone asks you what I said, tell them
To read your books, since mine is the human stem

That participates in the voice of all women
That takes root in you and from which derives
Your voice that channels many other lives.

I live in multiple brains but my being thrives
Particularly in yours, which is justified
By the love and compassion on which we both relied.

Together we looked at the sky and identified
The infinite, which for you became the first
Theory, which created in you a permanent thirst

That became redemptive when you faced the worse
And tried to redeem suffering that felt like a curse.
Though you gave up the religion of your youth,

That was sorting out falsehood from the truth.
Your philosophers of choice I may not have read,
But I know what they came to be in your head—

Another resurrection of the dead."

CANTO 31

"Now look around," she said, "at this green place—
Though good for a rest, it's not the source of grace,
For nothing's redeemed without joining the chase

For illusive truth with which we must keep pace
By confronting the gaps in what we think we know
That open our minds to the eternal flow

Of thought that can't remain in this limbo
Without its becoming a stagnant swamp—
Which for some people would be a joyous romp,

Wallowing in the mire—but we need to be prompt
And return to the place where this long dream began."
Then on that note as she took hold of my hand,

I felt myself translated by her command
To Pine and 34th Avenue in Seattle,
And my mind didn't bother to unravel

The mystery of how we were able to travel
From whatever place it was where we had been
To this place where I had had to begin

My journey, which I could not say just when
That was—a month, a week, a second ago.
It was like the lifetime I'd spent at a picture show

Before coming out to feel the sun's glow
As if for the first time, when I felt reborn
Into a new world no longer forlorn

Because imagination's power had borne
Me away on waves of unrelenting hope
That gave me a view to the unlimited scope

Of what people could be if they awoke
From the darkness of finitude that says being
Can never be more than what you're seeing

Canto 31

Here and now, so there's no point in dreaming.
Then my mother spoke: "Even as a boy when you stared
Into that tiny TV screen you bared

Yourself in a way that sometimes scared
Me because I could see how it spoke to you,
How it plumbed emotional depths that seemed taboo

In a child who should not have to feel so blue,
And I feared you would begin to hear noises,
The cacophony of incoherent voices

That began to echo in my head, boisterous,
But without any clarity, until the day
As one voice they told me to disobey

My common sense, and I resisted their sway
Because they seemed like devils out for my soul,
And taking yours might also be their goal,

But for you the voices played a different role,
And now I see fear was my true enemy.
Sometimes I dragged you away from that TV,

But began to see those shows had set you free
By giving you the strength to overcome
The cruelty to which your father would succumb

When he told you you'd always be a bum.
Yet the voices finally overwhelmed me,
And at first you felt betrayed because suddenly

You found yourself alone but a force heavenly—
Call it the power of imagination—
Directed your anger toward new creation

When you turned to books for liberation
And forgave my unintended violation
Of innocence that didn't know itself.

Comedy, Book Three

But it took years before you could dispel
The burden of trauma in that childhood hell."
Then I said, "There were lights along the way,

Each one a luminous Beatrice,
Because my love for you translated into
The love of all women that could undo

The cruel negations that I had lived through.
First to come was Patty's Catholic innocence,
Her gaze could not deflect my harsh dissonance,

But at least I learned to face my ambivalence—
Knowing I had hurt her became my penance.
Phyllis was the hard-headed woman from the song

Of Cat Stevens—she thought I was all wrong
And couldn't reciprocate my love but gave
The only love she could, for inside her cave

Were dark emotions and I didn't know how to save
Her from herself—dark on dark isn't right—
But her intellect lit the way through my night

And guided me through tempests like a sprite.
Karen's calm soul was the shade of a tree—not of
Good and evil but undemanding love—

In the end our lasting friendship was enough.
Mary Ann's love became her philosophy
When our souls touched with sublime curiosity

And I feasted on her generosity.
Mary Kay taught me the sensual arts,
And how lovers have to play multiple parts,

But from her I also learned that broken hearts
Emit a light that keeps the soul alive,
And lost love has the power to revive

Canto 31

Its own corpse when the other has arrived.
Mary Lou became the grand illusion,
And losing her I fell into confusion,

And almost missed the amorous revolution
When she finally came my way—you know her well
Because more than the others in her you dwell,

Though each love had the power to propel
Me toward the one whose love was the final shore.
They were teachers, the lovers who came before—

It's their own fault I had to love her more.
John Lennon was right, you never lose affection,
But the truest love is always the exception,

Forever something new in its progression."
At this my mother smiled and its radiance
Swept all clouds from the sky and arcadian

Light disrupted Seattle's circadian
Rhythms, which told me I was still in a dream,
For never before had this great city seemed

Such a paradise, and I asked what it must mean.
Her reply: "Heaven is only a point of view,
An infrequent state of mind that we pass through

When we give truth another turn of the screw—
Like once when you were young and feeling blue,
To a listening room at school you had to go

To hear Tchaikovsky's violin concerto,
And that music chased away sorrow,
And almost with tears you felt an ecstasy

And knew if this was all you'd ever be,
The recipient of this passing beauty,
It was worth it, it justified your life,

Comedy, Book Three

No matter how painful or full of strife.
Music is the human form divine,
For me the voice of God, but I can't define

What that means, perhaps just a feeling sublime
That causes us to lose all sense of time—
And death, love lost, abandonment, poverty,

These die into absolute equality,
Not everyone the same but incomparable.
Music speaks by saying the unsayable,

By any other means, unobtainable,
Though every art approaches this infinite ground
Even if its music is frozen sound.

In that ecstasy you were to heaven bound,
And every feeling of love had to resound
With the same truth, even when it led to pain,

Which to every true love is the refrain.
The one you love the most I love as well,
And unlike me she's not under the spell

Of dogma or psychological hell.
You both have sacrificed and compromised
In a long conversation that tells no lies,

Though in the process you're constantly surprised.
The things we do in life last forever,
And we all fall down when we think we'll never

Reach that absolute truth through our endeavor,
But time itself is the great forgiver
And death its agent lifts the veil of terror

That hides from us the necessity of error."

CANTO 32

"To me," I said, "the greatest terror today
 Is the multitude's willingness to betray
 Its own future when it chooses to give away

Democratic autonomy and obey
 The psychotic fantasies of some 'strong' man."
 Then my mother: "Power's an illusion, a brand,

That wealth burns into the sick mind of the band
 That imagines nothing against it can ever stand,
 Not multitude, not the forces of nature,

For they see themselves as the ultimate creator.
 Now rise with me to see what they create."
 Hand in hand we began to levitate

Until I saw the power to desolate
 My world with water that would inundate
 The heart of this city because too late

Came the political will to palliate
 The violence of wasteful consumption
 And challenge the capitalist subsumption

Of human creation and its presumption
 That nature is property for selling and buying.
 Then my mother spoke: "You see the waters rising

In a possible future not too surprising,
 But this is not the worse that can happen
 If we continue to be our own assassin—

I mean humankind that has a passion
 More for self-destruction than for self-love."
 Then from where we floated in the air above,

We saw Seattle return to itself enough
 To make me calm when suddenly a light
 Unbearable flashed and filled my soul with fright

Comedy, Book Three

As a mushroom cloud arose to a greater height
Than ours and then came oblivion's wind
That whipped us into the distance of time's end,

And eyes closed I prayed for forgiveness of sin,
Only to feel a sudden calm, then my eyes
Opened again and no more goodbyes

Haunted my world as I looked around and surmised
Everything was back in place like before.
Then we descended to an earth restored—

Not to perfection for what standard could accord
Us that—but to our human possibilities.
So my mother said, "Don't let our proclivities

For death hide the ground of our affinities,
The common or minimal consensus,
Without which all our languages are senseless,

Though indeed our errors can be tragically momentous.
One day it's possible we'll go too far
Or some minority become the star

And substitute for multitude a tsar
Whose madness negates all human existence—
But ends will come whatever our persistence,

Suns will nova or die without assistance
From the forms of life to which they once gave birth.
But while we continue on this planet earth,

Our duty is to pursue something of worth,
And when unforeseen consequences teach
Us that intentions can be betrayed by the reach

That exceeds the grasp, our process we must breach
Through a change of direction that sustains
The infinity of truth that always remains

Canto 32

Incomplete, like that transfinite domain
Mathematicians call Cantor's paradise,
And though that idea utterly defies

My understanding, once with my own eyes
With you by my side I stared into the sky's
Depths, immeasurable though still material

And the only word I could think of was 'miracle.'
We are infinities inside and out
And if I had been able to see through the dark cloud

Of fear that haunted me when voices so loud
Echoed through my brain, I would not have heard
Monsters but multitudes who might have conferred

On me a mental power undeterred
To tell the world what they were telling me—
That the greatest evil is the refusal to see,

To look away from the divine family,
From all the beauty and misery we create.
But death taught me that it's never too late,

The lives of my children and theirs will translate
My life into visionary discourse,
For in each of you I instilled an ethical force

Of which I cannot be the singular source.
Others speak through me as they also speak
Through you, though refracted by the prism oblique

Of my intellect, which to some may have seemed weak,
Even mad, but its aim was liberation
Of those who wore the chains of segregation,

Or those whose labor was exploitation,
Like your father, whose unflowered imagination
Warred against itself in constant negation,

Comedy, Book Three

Which for all of us became a tribulation.
But the goodness in him felt the ethical call
When like Jesus Christ he suffered for us all,

Even if around himself he built a wall.
Without him none of us would have survived,
And as he aged his spiritual self revived—

We all fall down but then sometimes we rise.
It has been your special task to write it down
In language to which your spirit has been bound,

And the record of this dream should be the crown,
Not as reward or honor but the part
Of your seed that strives toward the becoming of art,

Though no work is all art but a place to restart
The process that seeks infinity to chart.
You can do this if you concentrate the will,

But now it's time for us to descend this hill."
Down Pine and through trails between the homes,
Across a bridge in the Valley of the Gnomes,

Then down steps to a boulevard we roamed—
The street by the lake where once lived Kurt Cobain
With a bench in Viretta Park that speaks his name

In graffiti hieroglyphics that entertain
All the teen spirits that haunt this sad domain.
We sat and my mother spoke: "Before I leave

You for a while, I ask you to believe
In our common voice, and that each one of us
Has the power of thought that must command our trust—

I mean all human beings who know the just
And the unjust, even if they wander away
From the path or cannot find the words that say

Canto 32

What the beating heart tells them to obey—
And yes, at different times, they will betray
Their own truth when they're overcome with hate

Or pride or greed or worship of the state,
Or fear they'll be cast out as reprobate—
And sometimes fear of the voices made my head

Spin, which shrouded the heaven of thought with dread
Until spiritual joy was almost dead.
Oh I wish I could have been like William Blake

And communed with the voices like someone awake,
Not to submit but to challenge and explore
In a dialogue that could open a door

To new heavens of experience that store
All the infinities in the human brain.
But sometimes I came close and that must remain

My legacy against the source of pain
That only came from fear, the iron chain
Like the hand of death whose hold seems unbreakable

To us, and unconsciousness unwakable,
But every true thought is consciously awake
And cannot die but follows in time's wake

Because truth's essence means it cannot forsake
Anyone or it has not passed the test,
The universality of its address,

Which is a process that can never rest
For its prescriptions are only echoes
Of infinity and each by itself narrows

Truth's scope but is constantly redeemed as it goes
Through revisions that form the infinite set.
So I look back on my life without regret,

Comedy, Book Three

Since only the multitude can pay the debt
For all the errors for which I've too long wept.
Now I must go though my thought is in the air

You breathe, your share of universal care."

CANTO 33

As I watched her die into the atmosphere
With which she became one to form the frontier
Of my mental existence, I had to look down

To ponder those events that seemed profound
In a dream that might have been a living vision,
Though I was still wrapped in indecision.

But as I pursued this private inquisition,
I felt the presence of someone next to me
And turned slowly to face who it could be,

And almost laughed at what I had to see,
For to this quest what more perfect crescendo
Than the visitation of Marlon Brando,

But not in the flesh he wore when he was old
But the way he looked when he played Terry Malloy
In a movie on which I obsessed when I was a boy

With feelings both tragic and full of joy.
Then he spoke: "You and I have one thing in common,
My father said I'd always be a bum,

Which made me want to prove I was someone,
And you heard that history in the voice on the screen,
For into that act I put more than was seen

And in your brain there's a permanent trace of the scene
With the brother, you know the one I mean,
And for both of us the brother was the father,

Who made me an actor and you a scholar,
Though you never settled into that role
And I never found in acting my soul—

It turned out nothing we did could fill the hole
Our fathers dug to bury our self-esteem
And from the bottom sometimes would come the scream

Comedy, Book Three

Like the one in *Last Tango* almost obscene,
Because my best acting was not acting
When something was yanked out of me like extracting

An abscessed tooth with the visual grafting
Of the inner pain onto the imagined self,
But none of my performances ever felt

Like anything more than a con that dealt
A cheating hand in a game I couldn't stand."
Then I: "Once as a boy I thought I was damned

And dreamed eternal hellfire was God's plan
For me, and there was nothing psychiatry
Could do to banish the dark, savage poetry

That resembled what Dante Alighieri
Wrote and filled my nights with ungodly horror,
But literature wasn't my first restorer—

No, cinema was where like an explorer
Of human emotions I found a force divine
That exceeded religion with its more sublime

Vision of humanity that could combine
Good and evil in a complex design
That echoed the darkness and the light inside

And told me there was no reason to hide
From a truth process that fused pleasure and pain.
Though my words back then would not have been the same

As now, movies projected a profane
Illumination that fired the imagination
And led to a lifelong investigation

Of beauty and its constant violation
By the real that haunts our dreams of paradise.
So when Terry recreates the passion of Christ

Canto 33

And takes the long walk to regain his rights,
I saw courage with the power to redeem
The flesh that sometimes fails like a machine

But then through resurrection unforeseen
Transcends itself to become a beautiful one.
Yet when I thought the human spirit had won,

I read Budd Schulberg's novel that like a gun
Pointed at my head replaced the joy with dread
Because at the end Terry Malloy was dead

In a barrel of lime, and that sinister thread
Was spun into the fabric of my thought,
And though at first I felt like someone caught

In a trap, another recognition brought
Me to a brighter illumination of truth—
Like when Blake followed the innocence of youth

With cruel experience that felt like a coup
Until this dialectical image revealed
The unity blind innocence concealed.

Good's only reward is the justice it must yield,
But the war against evil remains the same.
I know that Schulberg and Kazan named names,

And some would say this blights the movie's fame
But truth has no author to take the blame,
And the singularity of the work of art

Comes not from the author but the infinite part
That transforms the errors of the human heart
Into a force that touches the absolute,

The voice of multitudes that can't pollute
But only expand the breadth of aesthetic truth."
Then Brando: "Some say my career went awry

Comedy, Book Three

After *Waterfront*, and I guess they don't lie,
But Hollywood wasn't my paradise,
And I got tired of having to pay the price

For a talent that to them was merchandise.
Then they called my politics the acts of a fool—
Well, I didn't go to a finishing school

Of public relations and the lord of misrule
Often reigned in my head, but I really did care
About the First Nations who deserved a share

Of the wealth and freedom that a millionaire
Like me got so easily, which ain't quite right
When the same doesn't go for all the not-white—

But as your James Joyce might say, isn't that shite?
Isn't color coding humans a blight?
Maybe I was some kind of hypocrite,

But this much about me you'll have to admit—
Fool that I was, I never looked away,
Not like these jokers who steal the stage today

Aiming to make billions when they choose to betray
Their craft for a buck—and then don't give a fuck!
To hell with anyone who's out of luck!"

Then I: "No one should say you ran amok.
Actors like De Niro, Pacino, DiCaprio,
Nicholson, and so many others all owe

You such a debt that time can only grow—"
But before I finished, I heard, "Adios, amigo!"
And as a misty rain began to fall

I saw him drift away beyond recall,
And I knew I was awake again in Seattle
Sitting on a wet bench after having traveled

Canto 33

Through lightyears of unconsciousness unraveled
By imagination, and these thoughts came to me:
Walking the streets of more than one city,

I had touched the physical form of community,
The living organism of multitude,
And even when I suffered solitude,

I felt the pulse of human beatitude,
The divine force of love that creates a home,
The only paradise the earth has grown,

The only absolute that time has thrown
Onto the path we fear we'll endlessly roam.
But home embraces totality of space,

Without borders, without exclusions or waste
Of human compassion or imagination—
And the dream of a democratic nation

Cannot be realized through the domination
Of wealth or the construction of a wall
That tries to shut out the being of the all.

Every storm that comes will issue the call
To join forces against another fall.
But now I thought of the one who shared my life

In the best of times or in the times of strife,
And her image directed my steps like a guide,
Leading me out of the mind's helter skelter

With wandering steps back to our common shelter.

End of *Comedy*
Seattle, Washington 2017–2024

NOTES

CANTO 1: Place: Memphis, Tennessee. **Furry Lewis and Bukka White:** 20th Century blues guitarists and singers. **Sun Records:** Recording studio and label that initially recorded African-American blues artists and later rising white artists like Elvis Presley and Johnny Cash. **Nathan Bedford Forrest:** Confederate Army general and first Grand Wizard of the Ku Klux Klan. **strange fruit:** from the protest song against lynching sung by Billie Holiday with the line: "Southern trees bear a strange fruit." **Firbolg:** legendary neolithic inhabitants of Ireland, sometimes described as bagmen, slaves, commoners. **what Joni did to Furry:** Joni Mitchell's "Furry Sings the Blues." **judges would be in a penitentiary too:** Furry Lewis's "Judge Harsh Blues" with the lines: "Judge all talking 'bout what they will do / If they had justice he'd be in penitentiary too." **Dylan . . . named it Memphis:** Bob Dylan's "Stuck Inside of Mobile with the Memphis Blues Again." **Lennon / Cried out . . . :** John Lennon's "Mother."

CANTO 2: Place: Memphis. **Been down so long:** Richard Farina's novel *Been Down So Long It Looks Like Up to Me*. **southern man Neal Young debunked:** Neal Young's "Southern Man." *if the river was whiskey*: Furry Lewis's "I Will Turn Your Money Green." **Pat Smith:** owner of The Last Laugh.

CANTO 3: Place: Memphis. **Charybdis chasm:** a monstrous whirlpool in Homer's *Odyssey*. *[We] Gotta get out of this place*: The Animals' song. *binding with briars, my joys & desires*: Blake's "The Garden of Love."

CANTO 4: Place: Memphis. **Historical Figure: Richard Wright,** with references to his autobiography, *Black Boy*. **Rosa Luxemburg:** Polish-German Marxist activist and theorist, murdered by right-wing paramilitaries during the Spartacist Uprising in Germany (1919). **Ralph Ellison:** African-American author of *Invisible Man*.

CANTO 5: Place: Memphis. **Historical Figure:** Wright. **John Lennon . . . on loves past:** see Canto 31 notes. **'Nobody knows my name':** the title of a collection of essays by James Baldwin.

NOTES

CANTO 6: Place: Memphis—New York City. **Historical Figure:** Wright. **Film:** John Schlesinger's *Midnight Cowboy* (1969). **Stonewall:** Stonewall Uprising in Greenwich Village on June 28, 1969, a foundational event for the Gay Rights Movement. **Sparts:** Spartacist League (SL), in 1970 a small sect of American Trotskyites, named after the German *Spartakusbund* of Rosa Luxemburg and Karl Liebknecht. **Robertson:** Jim Robertson, one of the founders and longtime head of SL.

CANTO 7: Place: New York City. **Historical Figure:** Robertson. **Nick:** member of SL in 1970.

CANTO 8: Place: New York City. **Historical Figure:** Robertson. **'the free development / Of individualities':** Marx's *Grundrisse*, the 1857-8 notebooks.

CANTO 9: Place: New York City. **Films:** Martin Scorsese's *Mean Streets* (1973) and *Gangs of New York* (2002). **mind-forged manacle:** Blake's poem "London." **Paradise Square:** located in the Five Points district of mid-nineteenth-century New York, recreated in *Gangs*. **Scorsese's expression of loss . . . :** at the end of *Gangs*, the quoted lines are the voiceover of Leonardo di Caprio's character. **Church Street Station:** USPS. **Stonewall:** see Canto 6 notes.

CANTO 10: Place: New York City. **Historical Figure:** John Lennon. **god tree:** the type of tree under which the Buddha achieved enlightenment. **the I is other . . . / As Rimbaud surmised:** "Je est un autre," which Rimbaud wrote in a letter at 16. **Like John Lennon sang:** The Beatles' "I Am the Walrus." *potentia:* Spinoza's Latin term for the diffuse power of the multitude as the foundation of all power. **I'm a loser:** Beatles' song.

CANTO 11: Place: New York City. **Historical Figure:** Lennon. **you can't tell heaven from hell:** Pink Floyd's "Wish You Were Here" with the lines: "so you think you can tell / Heaven from hell." **how the concept of God measures our pain:** see Canto 13.

CANTO 12: Place: New York City. **Historical Figure:** Lennon. *esse est Deus:* literally, "to be is God," to express the idea that being or existence is divine.

CANTO 13: Place: New York City—Chicago. **Historical Figure:** Lennon. **Film:** The Wachowskis' *The Matrix*, starring Keanu Reeves. **"God is a concept . . . ":** Lennon's song "God." **whatever gets you through . . . is all right:**

Lennon's song "Whatever Gets You Thru the Night." **Chums of Chance:** absurd characters from Thomas Pynchon's (**Tom**) novel *Against the Day*.

CANTO 14: Place: Chicago—Santa Cruz (University of California, UCSC). **Historical Figure: Norman O. Brown** (**Nobby**), professor at UCSC, author of *Life Against Death* and *Love's Body*. **Finnegans wake redeemed:** James Joyce's *Finnegans Wake*, where the Finnegans are common people or the multitude.

CANTO 15: Place: Santa Cruz. **Historical Figure:** Brown. *Aufhebung*: German word used by Marx, often translated with respect to capitalism as some form of "abolishing" but also carries the sense of "preserving or transcending." **en caul:** the birth of fetus with placenta, both covered by the amniotic sac.

CANTO 16: Place: Santa Cruz. **Historical Figure:** Brown. **Negri:** Antonio Negri, the Italian Marxist associated with *autonomia*, the worker's autonomy movement. In response to Marxist critiques of reformism, he wrote in *Time for Revolution*: "the ontological grounds of reformism have a real consistency."

CANTO 17: Place: Santa Cruz. **Historical Figures:** Brown and **Michael Cimino**, American film director. **Films:** Cimino's *Heaven's Gate* (1980), Sam Peckinpah's *Pat Garrett and Billy the Kid* (1973), Sergio Leone's *Once Upon a Time in the West* (1968) and *Once Upon a Time in America* (1984). **Beulah:** Blake's concept of an earthly paradise but also a place of rest from the Edenic wars of eternity, sometimes associated with the unconscious where contraries are equally true. **Jameson:** Fredric Jameson, leading American Marxist scholar, author of *The Political Unconscious*. **'Without contraries is no progression':** Blake's *The Marriage of Heaven and Hell*. **a war . . . between the rich and the poor:** the Johnson County War in Wyoming (1892) between the Wyoming Stock Growers' Association and small cattlemen, the subject of Cimino's film. **Bertolucci:** Bernardo Bertolucci, Italian film director. **an eye . . . we see through, not with:** Blake's poem "The Everlasting Gospel" when he refers to believing "a Lie / When you see with not thro the Eye." **Jim Averill (actual name Averell), Ella Watson, Nate Champion:** fictional characters in *Heaven's Gate*, whose names, but not their stories in every detail, derive from historical figures. **Heaven's Gate / Got cut . . . :** scene of community celebration in a building with the same name as the film.

NOTES

CANTO 18: Place: Santa Cruz—Paris. **Historical Figure:** Vincent Van Gogh. **Blake's prophecy, nothing is lost:** *Jerusalem*, with the lines "for not one Moment / Of Time is lost, nor one Event of Space unpermanent / But all remain."

CANTO 19: Place: Paris. **Historical Figures:** Van Gogh and **Michel Foucault,** French philosopher-historian, member of the Collège de France, author of *History of Madness, Discipline and Punish*, and numerous other works. **'There is peace even in the storm':** Van Gogh's letters. **bricks / In the wall:** Pink Floyd's "Another Brick in the Wall." **Gramsci's communism:** Antonio Gramsci, Italian communist, imprisoned by the fascists in the 1920s, to whom is attributed the phrase, "Pessimism of the intellect, optimism of the will," which he borrowed from French author Romain Rolland. **Alain Badiou:** French philosopher, author of *Being and Event, Logics of Worlds*, and *The Immanence of Truths*.

CANTO 20: Place: Paris. **Historical Figure:** Foucault. **Lacan:** Jacques Lacan, influential French psychoanalytic theorist. **the non-duped err:** Lacan's *Seminaire XXI*.

CANTO 21: Place: Paris. **Historical Figures:** Foucault and **Jacques Derrida,** celebrated French philosopher, who during my Fulbright year in 1982-83 lectured at the École Normal Supérieure, author of *Of Grammatology, Dissemination, Glas, The Postcard*, and numerous other significant works. **Film:** Alfred Hitchcock's *The Birds* (1963). **the murder of crows . . . in Hitchcock's dream:** scene in *The Birds*. The word "murder" here means "flock." **jouissance:** for Lacan, an ecstasy beyond pleasure and allied to the death drive. **Julia Kristeva:** Bulgarian-French philosopher, author of *Revolution in Poetic Language* and *Powers of Horror*. **passion of Inexistance:** Badiou's *Logics*, where it is spelled with an "a" instead of an "e" to suggest that what is inexistent in one world or context can have a full existence elsewhere and may even force the appearance of such a world or context.

CANTO 22: Place: Paris. **Historical Figure:** Derrida. **Antonio Negri:** see Canto 16 notes. **es gibt:** in German "there is" but literally "it gives" (see Derrida's *Given Time*). **déclaration de guerre:** declaration of war. **secular gospel of Mick:** The Rolling Stones' "Gimme Shelter." **Badiou:** see Canto 19 notes. **'communionism':** *Finnegans Wake*.

CANTO 23: Place: Paris. **Historical Figure:** Derrida. **Bourdieu:** French sociologist, member of Collège de France, author of *Distinction*. **nostalgérie:**

NOTES

portmanteau word, combining the French words for nostalgia and Algeria. ***Le Rouge et le Noir*:** Stendhal's masterpiece, with the characters Julien Sorel and Madame de Renal. **Emma Bovary:** Gustave Flaubert's *Madame Bovary.* **habitus:** in Bourdieu's sociology, learned preferences and dispositions that shape a person's relation to the social world. **Joyce's *seim anew*:** same or seme (basic unit of meaning) anew, *Finnegans Wake*. **novel Graham Greene wrote:** *The End of the Affair*.

CANTO 24: Place: Paris—Norman, Oklahoma (**OU:** University of Oklahoma). **Historical Figure:** Derrida. **Film:** John Ford's *The Searchers* (1956). **Osage people:** the Osage Nation bought their land in the Indian Territory (Oklahoma) in 1870 after selling their land in Kansas. As a result, when oil was discovered on their property, they had legal ownership of it. **black folk / In Tulsa:** Black Wall Street massacre of 1921.

CANTO 25: Place: Norman—Baton Rouge, Louisiana. **Film:** Florian Henckel von Donnersmarck's *Never Look Away* (2018, English title). **shroud of Turin:** linen cloth, in the Cathedral of St. John the Baptist in Turin with the faint image of a man's face on front and back, presumed to be the burial shroud of Jesus.

CANTO 26: Place: Baton Rouge (**LSU:** Louisiana State University). **Film:** Frank Darabont's *The Shawshank Redemption* (1994). **Joyce's Finnegans:** See Canto 14 notes. **John** and **John:** former LSU professors. **scene / Of his return:** see Book 2, Cantos 32-33.

CANTO 27: Place: Baton Rouge.

CANTO 28: Place: Baton Rouge and Blake's Beulah (see Canto 17 notes). **Film:** Scorsese's *Taxi Driver*. **De Niro's / Character:** Travis Bickle. **Sylviane:** Sylviane Finck, my former graduate student, who was murdered by her husband. Her dissertation has the primary title, *Reading Trauma in Modern and Postcolonial Literature*. **Like Mick Jagger sang:** The Rolling Stones' "(I Can't Get No) Satisfaction."

CANTO 29: Place: Beulah. **Films:** Scorsese's *Gangs of New York* and *Goodfellas* (1990) [**dark history of his own great city**], *Raging Bull* (1980) [**violence of wild masculinity**], *Alice Doesn't Live Here Anymore* (1974) [**women trapped...**], *Cape Fear* (1991) [**monsters bred from...poverty**], *The Aviator* (2004) [**power of capital ...**], *Shutter Island* (2006) [**killers can be saints**], *The Age of Innocence* (1993) [**aristocrats gangsters**], *Silence*

(2016) [**The harder lesson in imitation of Christ**], *The Last Temptation of Christ* (1988) [**Jesus had to struggle against . . . self-righteousness**], *Casino* (1995) [**that cathedral of cash**], *The Wolf of Wall Street* (2013) [**drunken hosannas to . . . plutocracy**], *The Irishman* (2019) [**the tragedy of organized labor**], *Kundun* (1997) and *Hugo* (2011) [**Dalai Lama And Méliès . . . The saint and the artist**]. "To live as a monster or die as a good man": *Shutter Island*. **contrapasso:** in Dante's *Commedia*, the principle that every punishment should reflect the sin it punishes. **Jesus's 'doubt and pain' . . . :** The Rolling Stones' "Sympathy For the Devil." **painted black:** The Rolling Stones' "Paint It Black." **Charlotte Delbo:** in the French resistance during World War 2, spent time at Auschwitz and other camps and later wrote about the experience and its psychological effect in her trilogy *Auschwitz and After*. **Philip Pullman:** author of fantasy novels with a philosophical edge such as *His Dark Materials* trilogy.

CANTO 30: Place: Beulah. **Not how things are but that they are . . . [is] the mystical:** Wittgenstein's *Tractatus Logico-Philosophicus*.

CANTO 31: Place: Beulah—Seattle. **John Lennon . . . you never lose affection:** The Beatles' "In My Life" with the lines: "Tho' I know I'll never lose affection / For people and things that went before."

CANTO 32: Place: Seattle. **Valley of the Gnomes:** a steep valley with a wooden bridge over it that extends East Pine Street between Madrona Drive and Evergreen Place in Seattle.

CANTO 33: Place: Seattle. **Historical Figure: Marlon Brando,** considered by many, myself included, to be the greatest film actor of all time, though his career was full of ups and downs. **Films:** Elia Kazan's *On the Waterfront* (1954) and Bernardo Bertolucci's *Last Tango in Paris* (1971). **Budd Schulberg:** wrote the screenplay for Kazan's movie and then wrote the novel version entitled simply *Waterfront*, in which there are significant differences from the film. **named names:** both Schulberg and Kazan gave names to the House Un-American Activities Committee.

www.ingramcontent.com/pod-product-compliance
Lightning Source LLC
Chambersburg PA
CBHW060519090426
42735CB00011B/2296